THE WONDERS OF NATURE

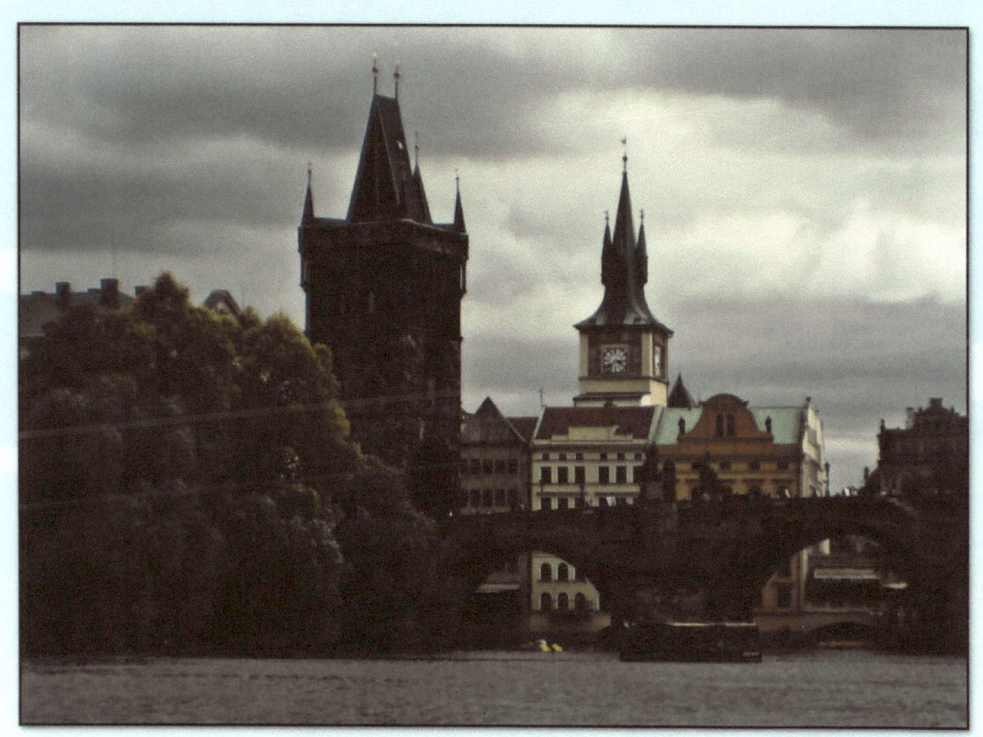

BY KATHLEEN ODENTHAL

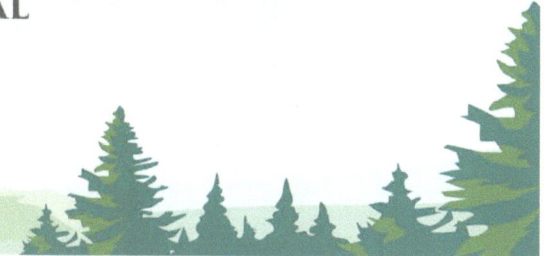

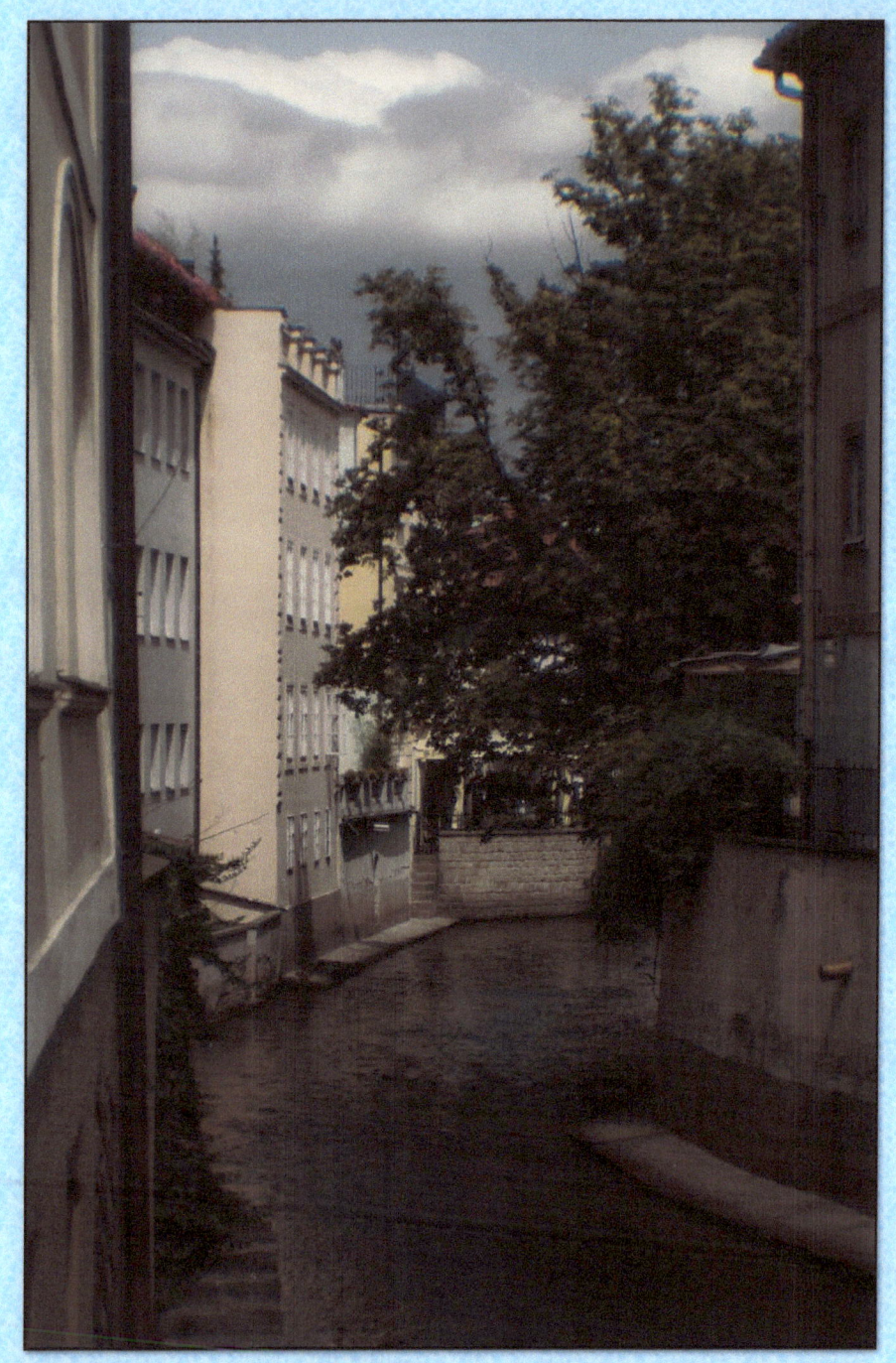

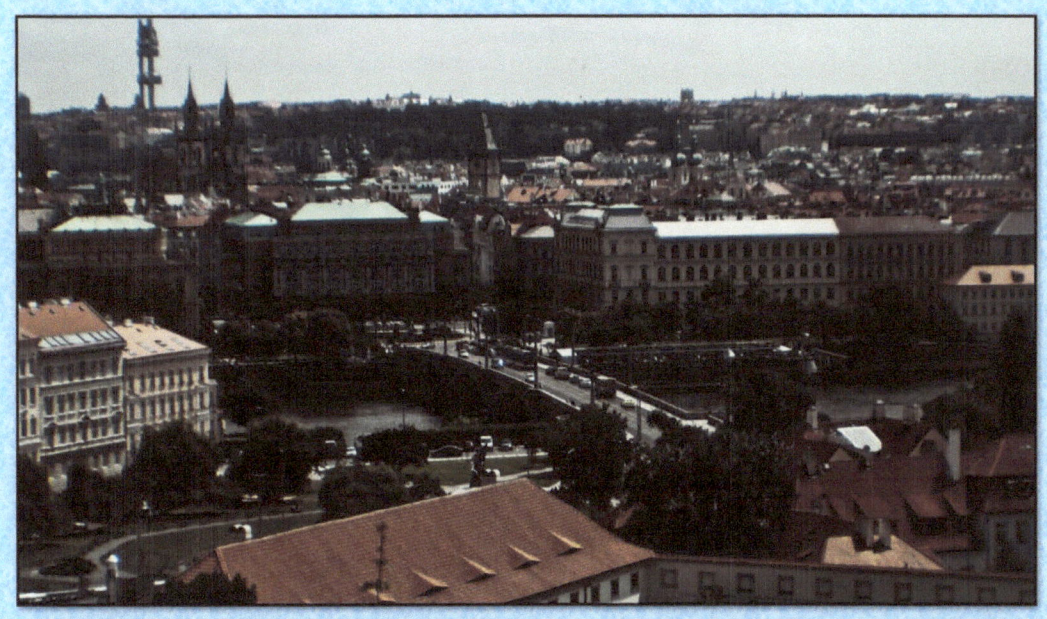

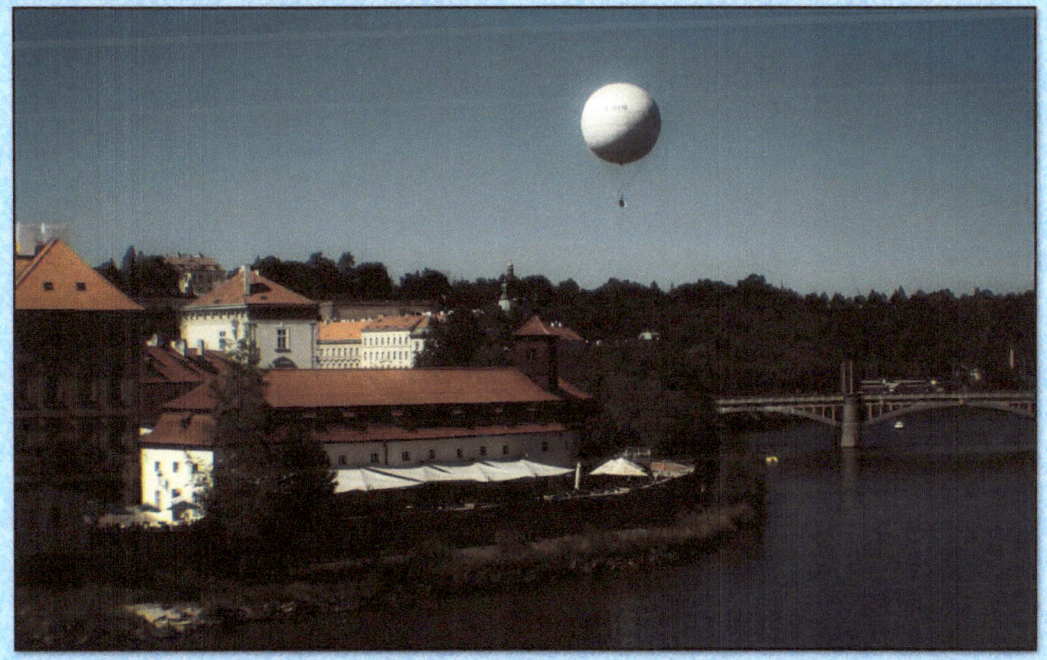

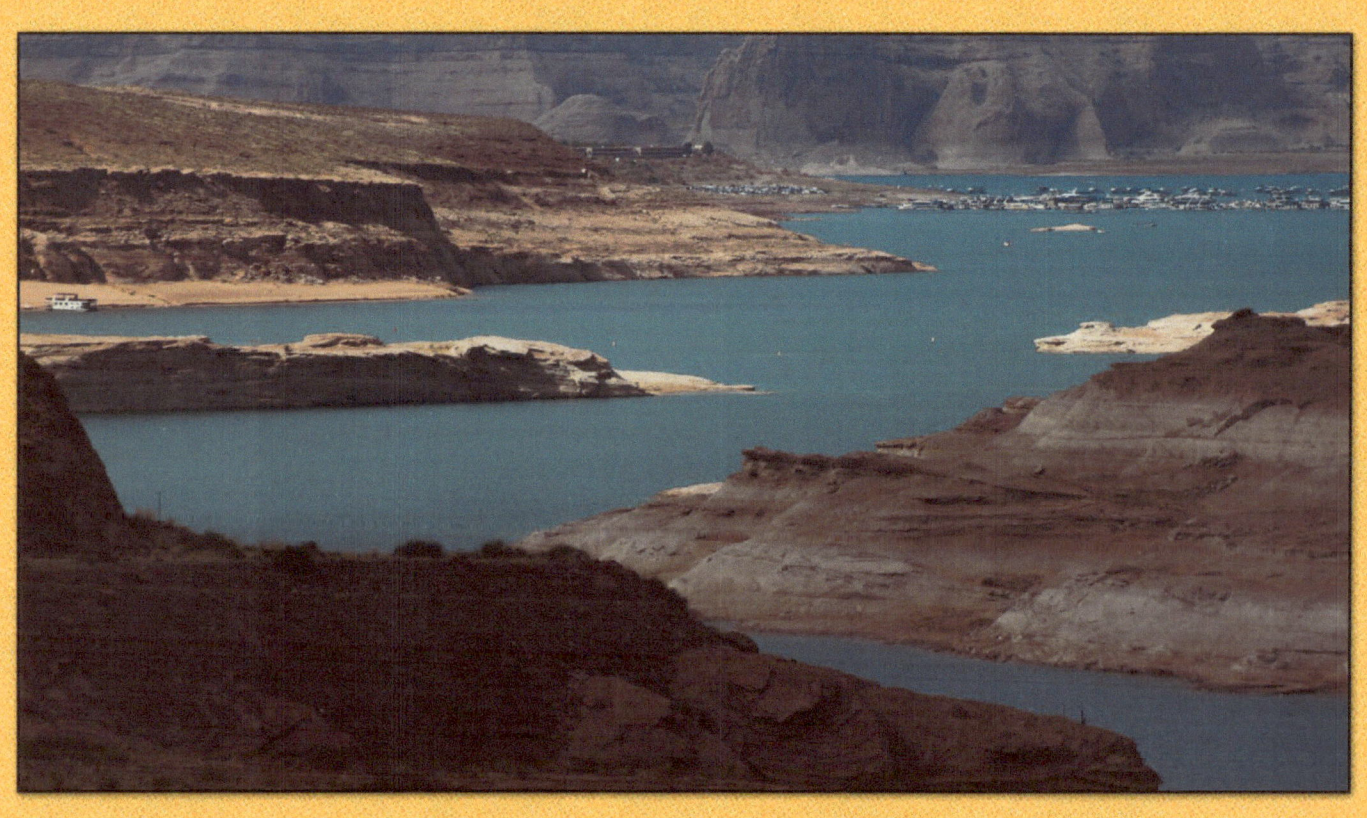

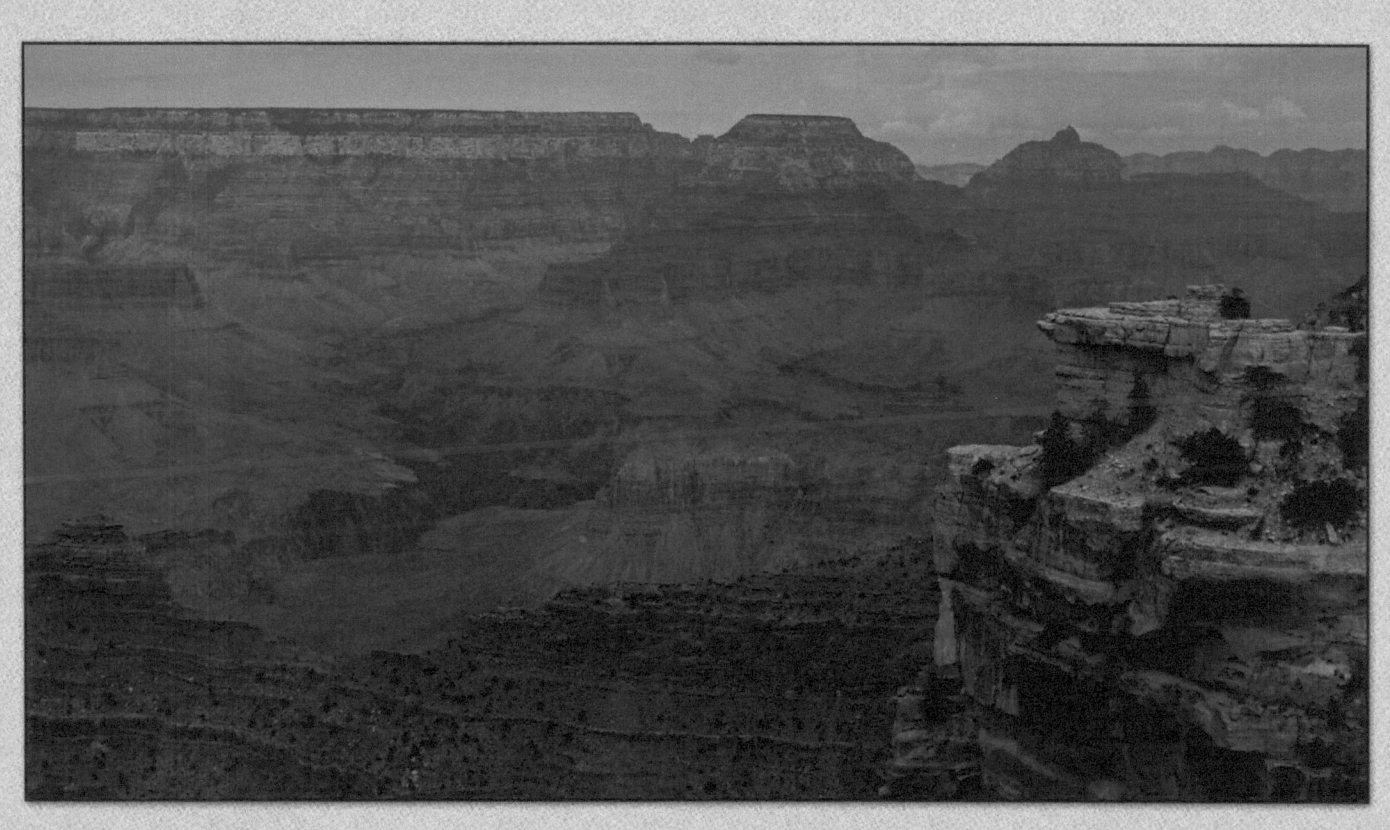

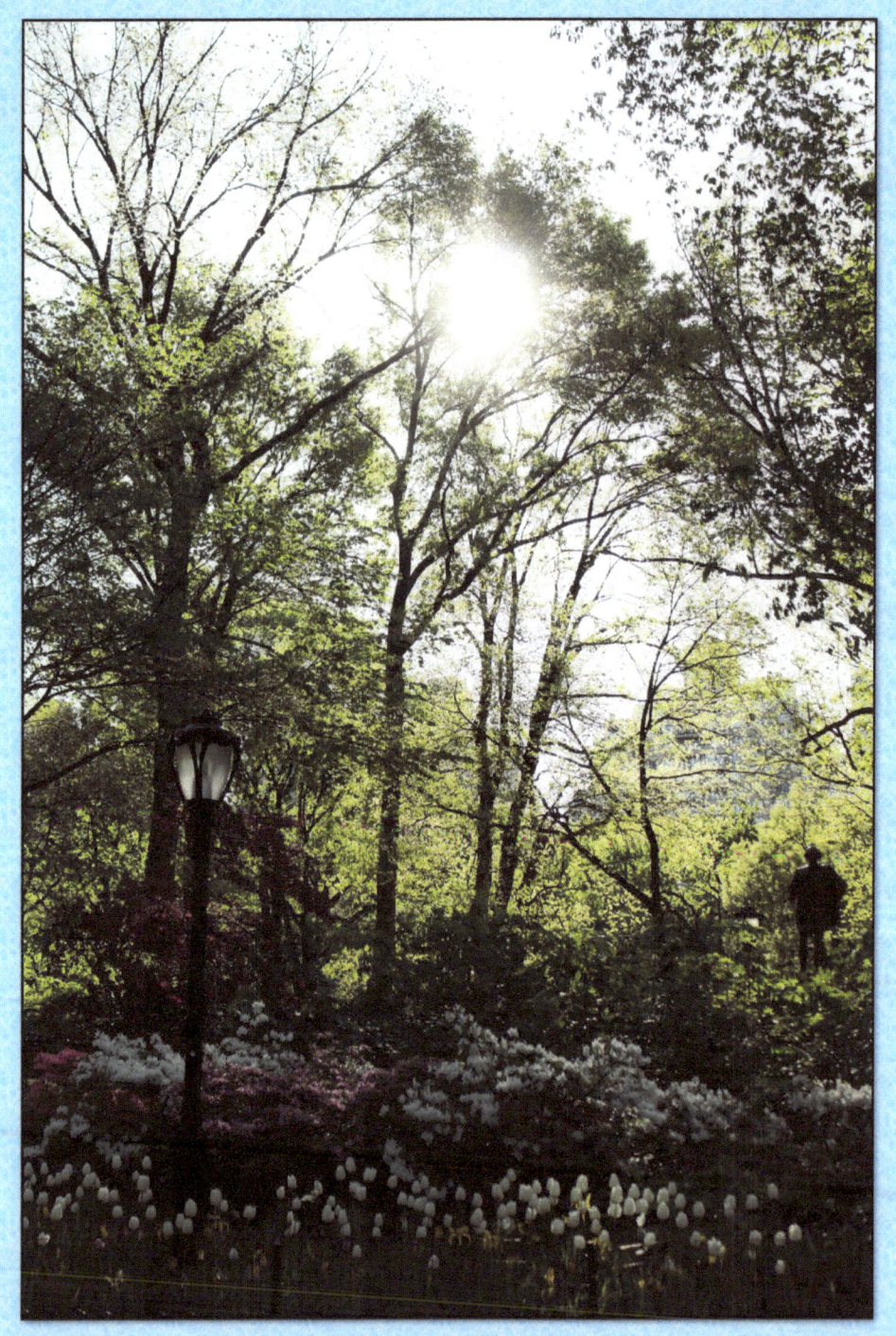

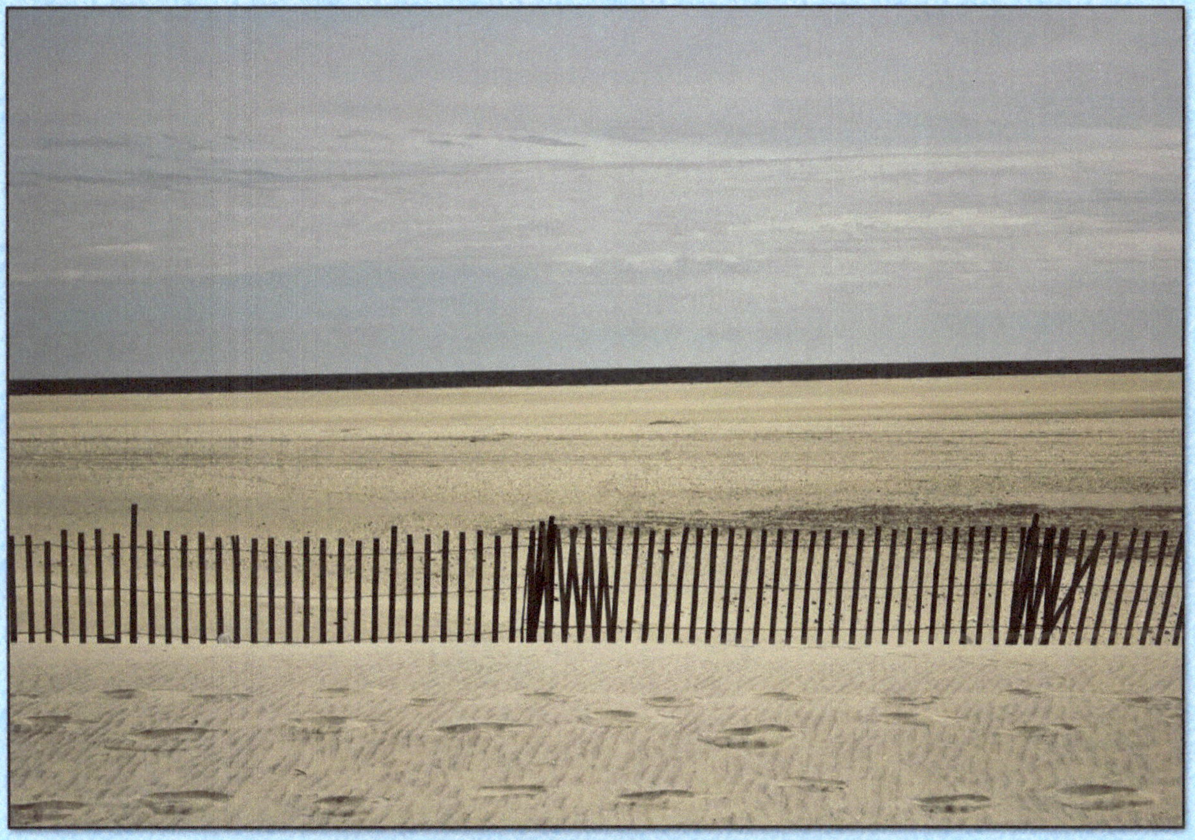

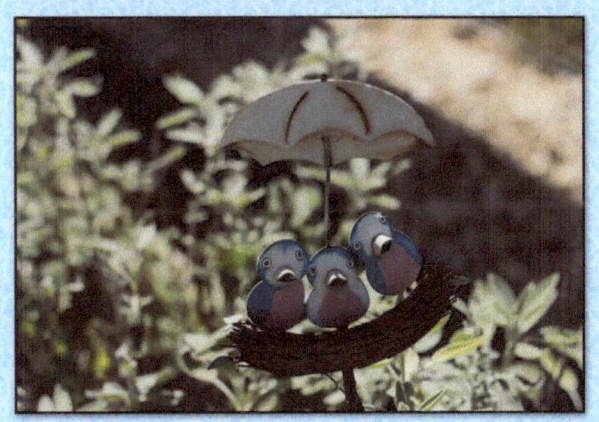

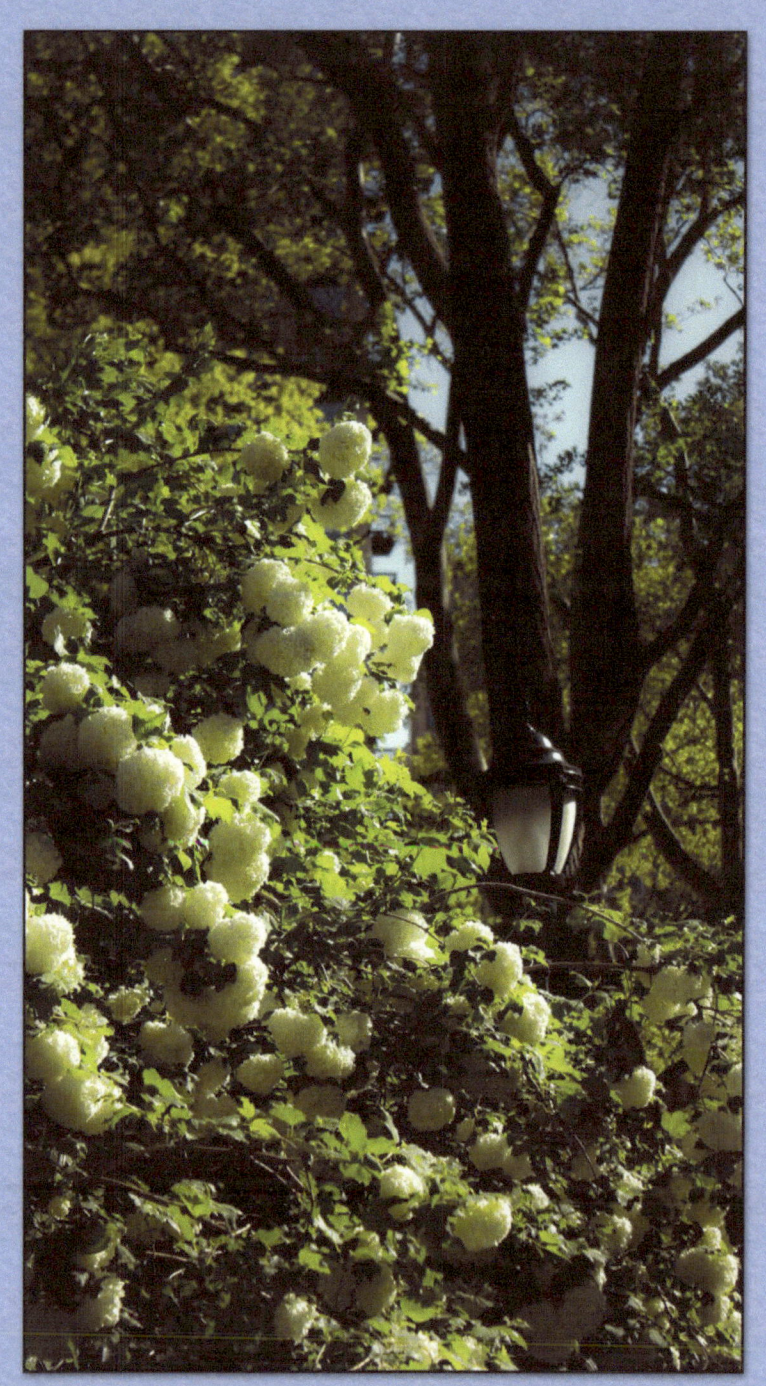

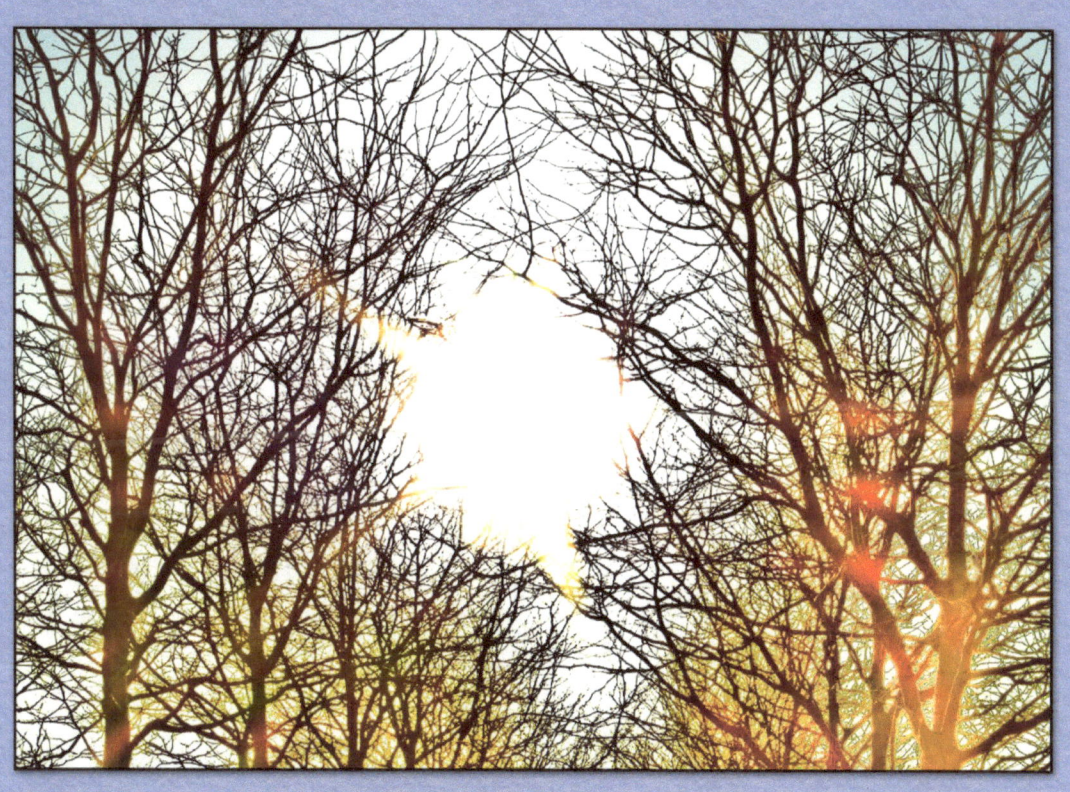

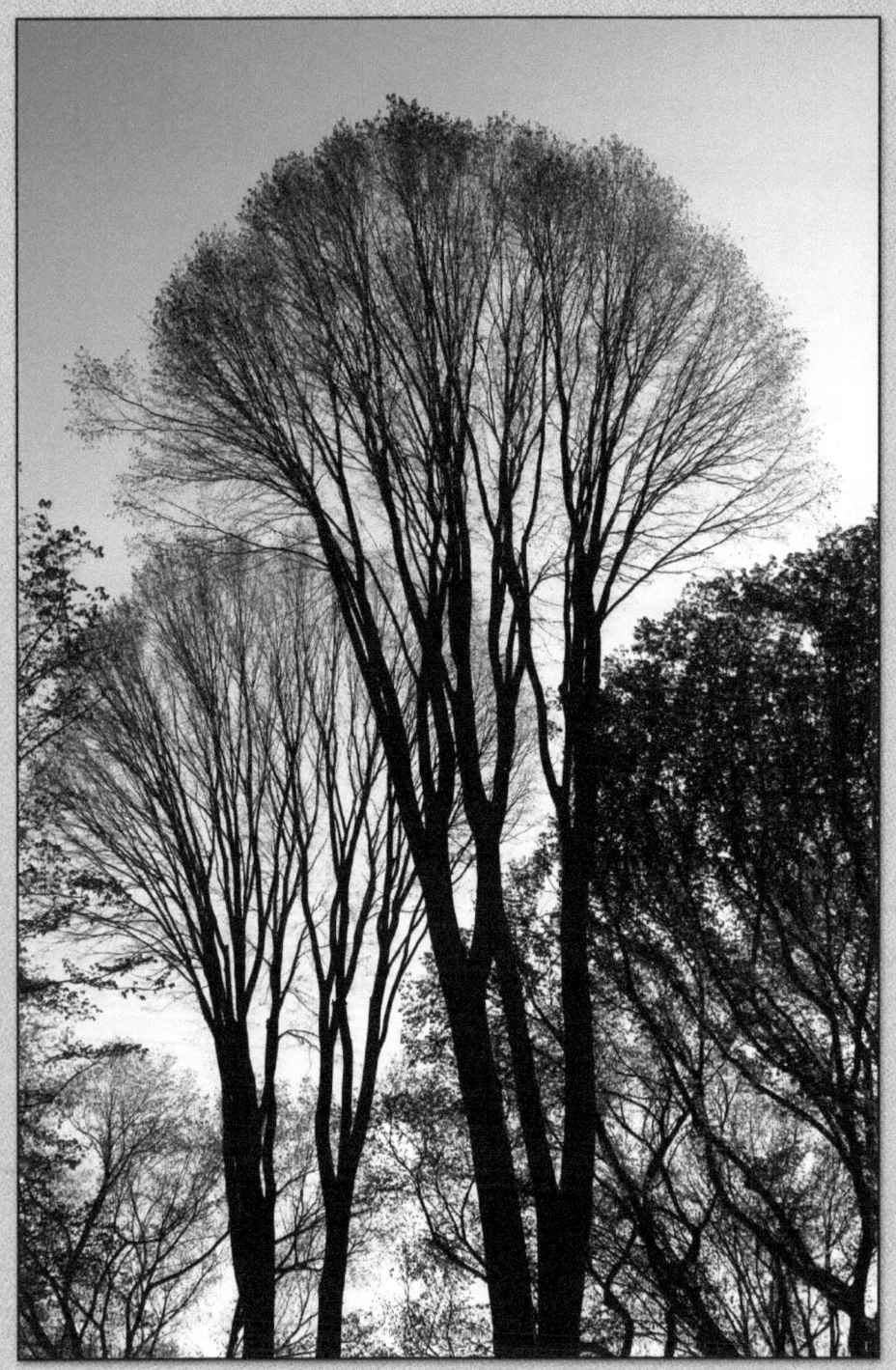

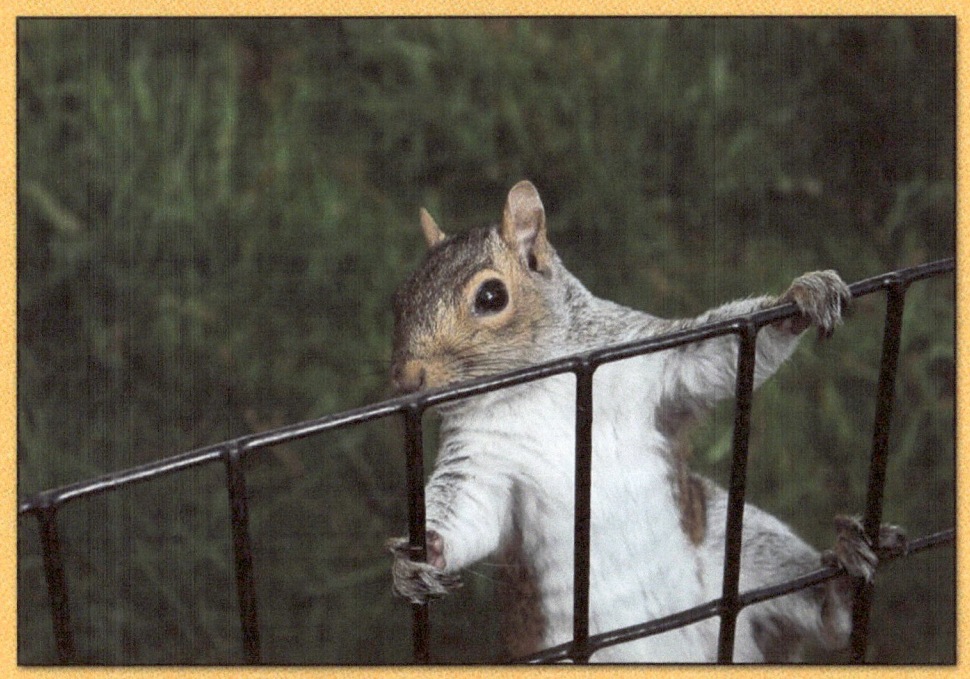

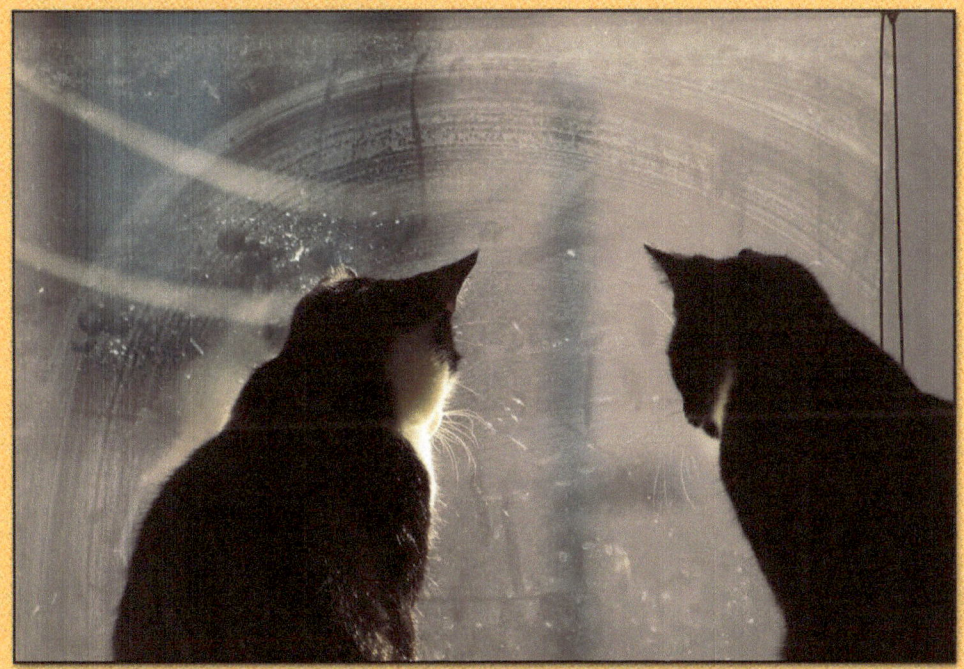

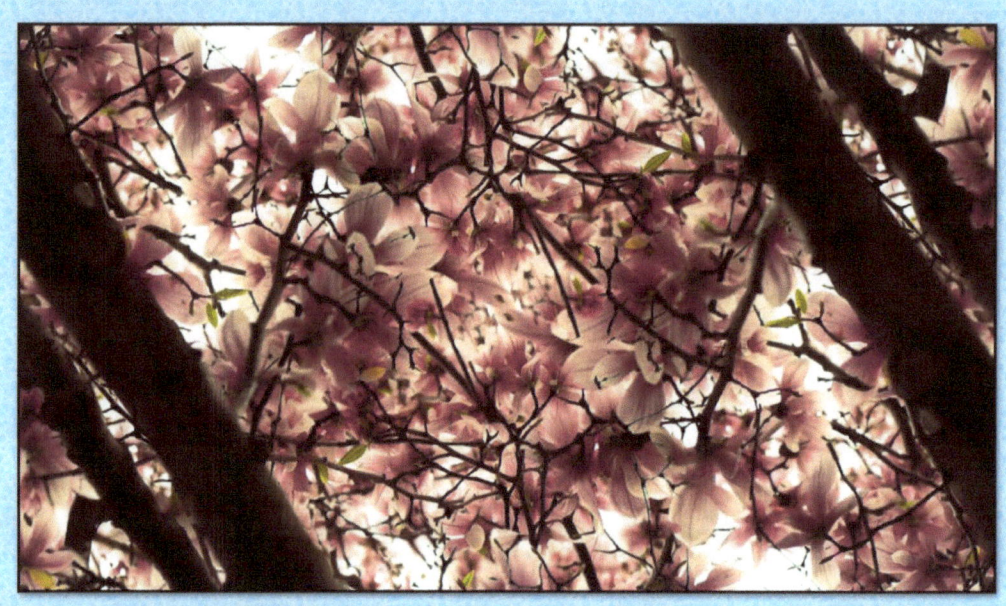

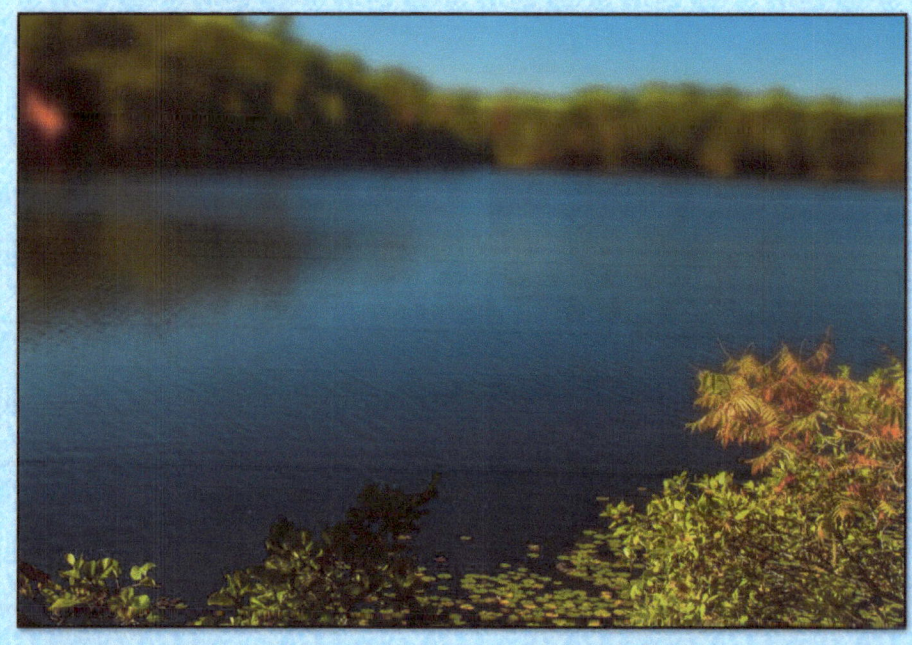

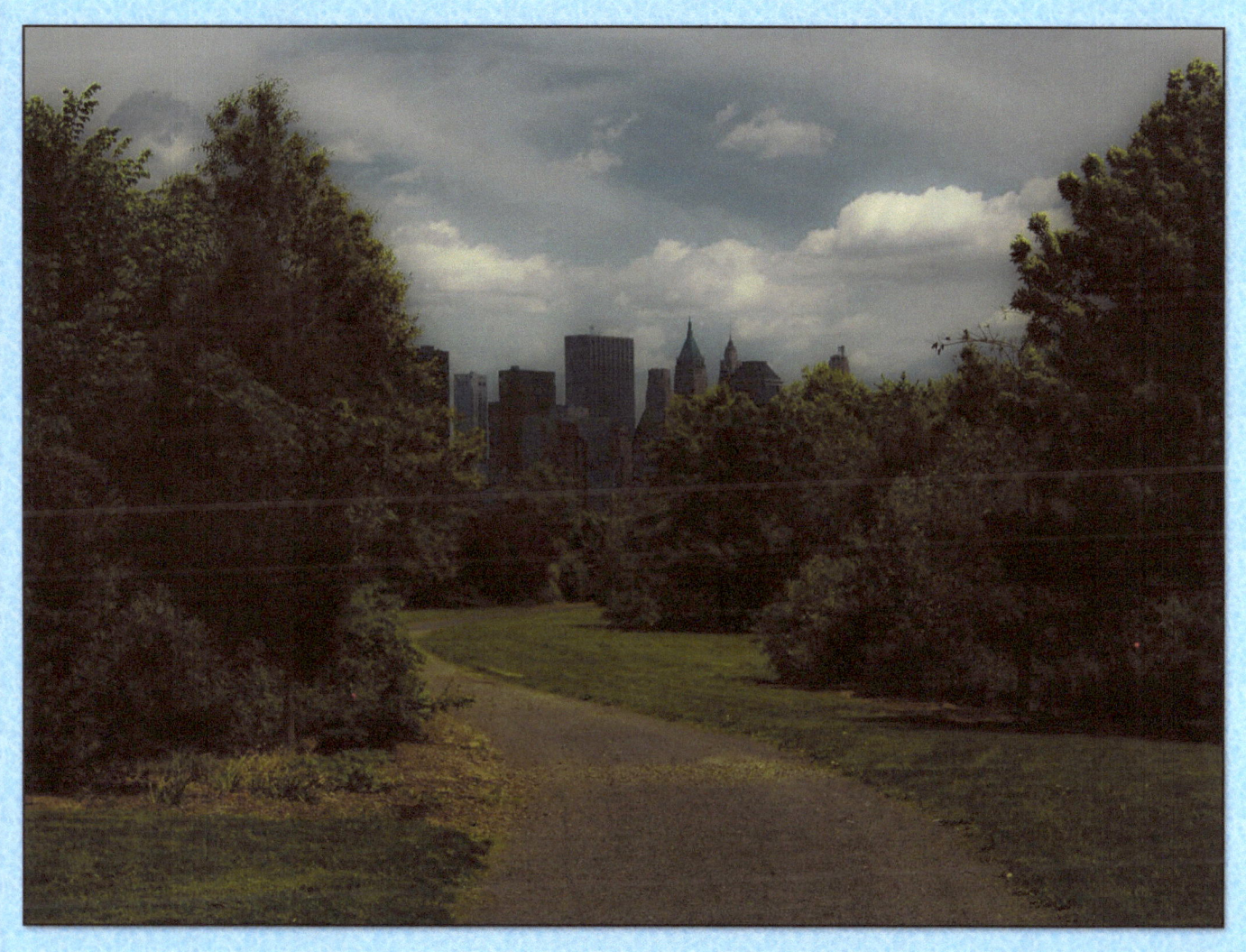

Title Here

Caption Here

Caption Here

Caption Here

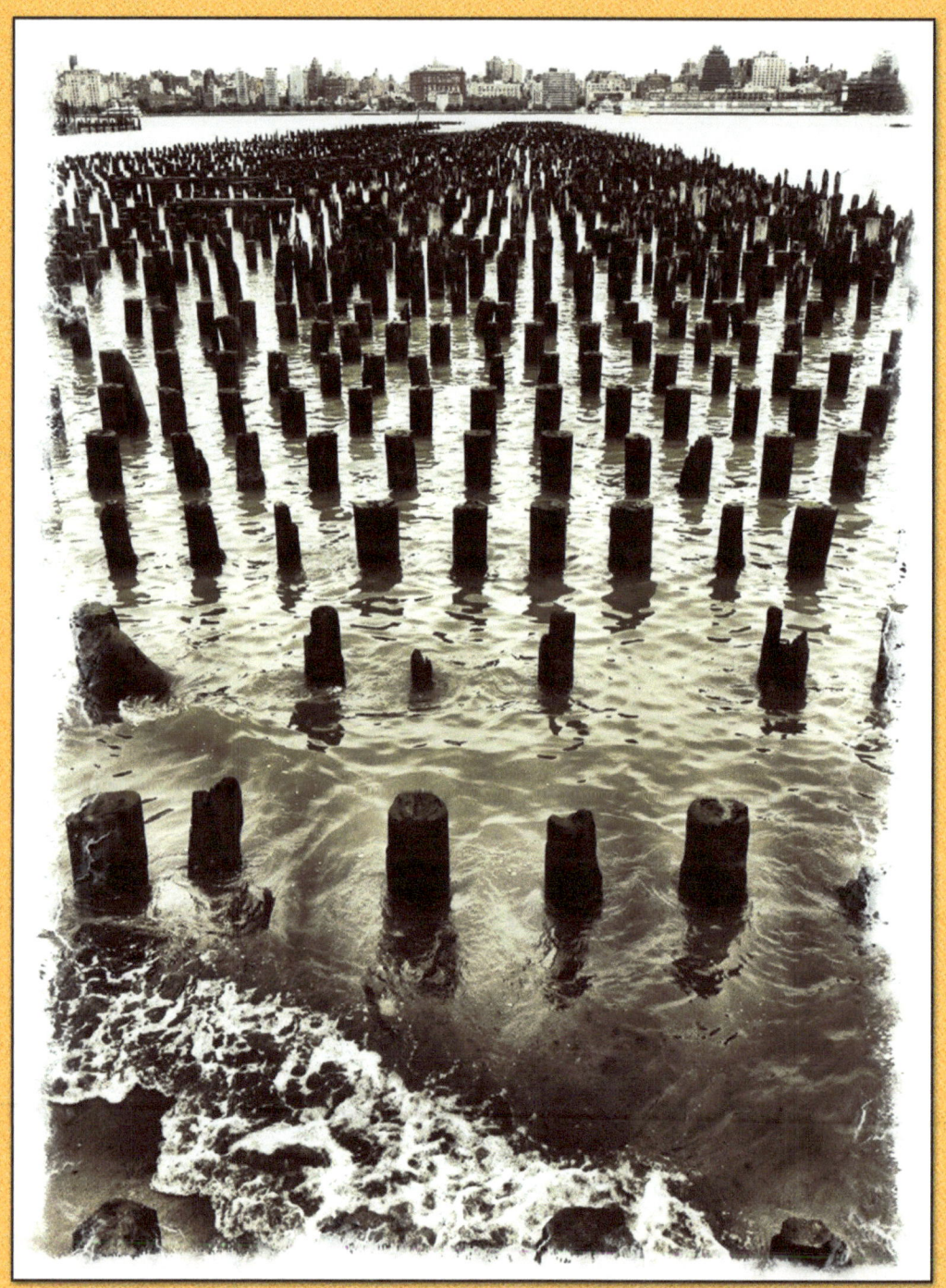

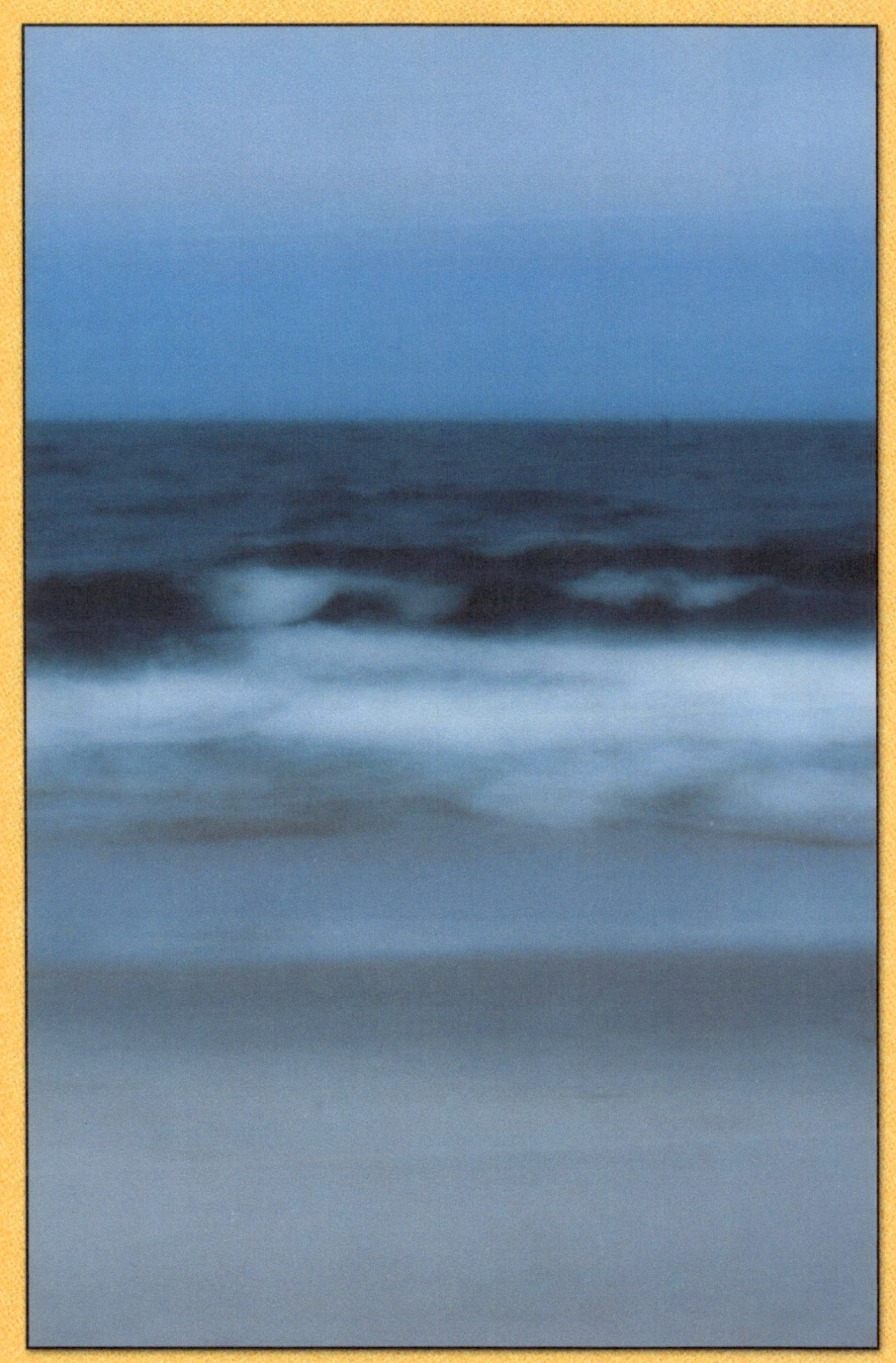

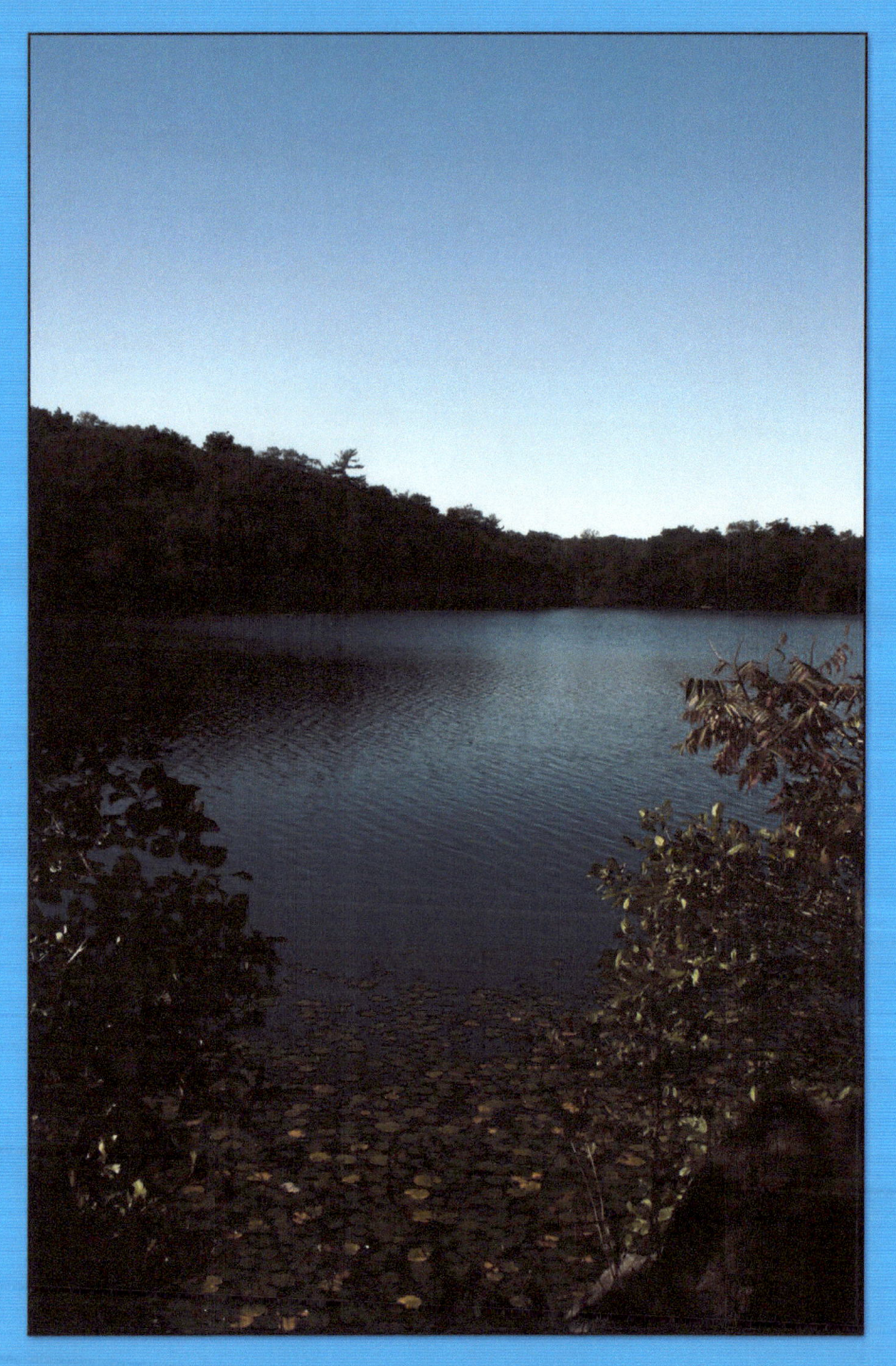

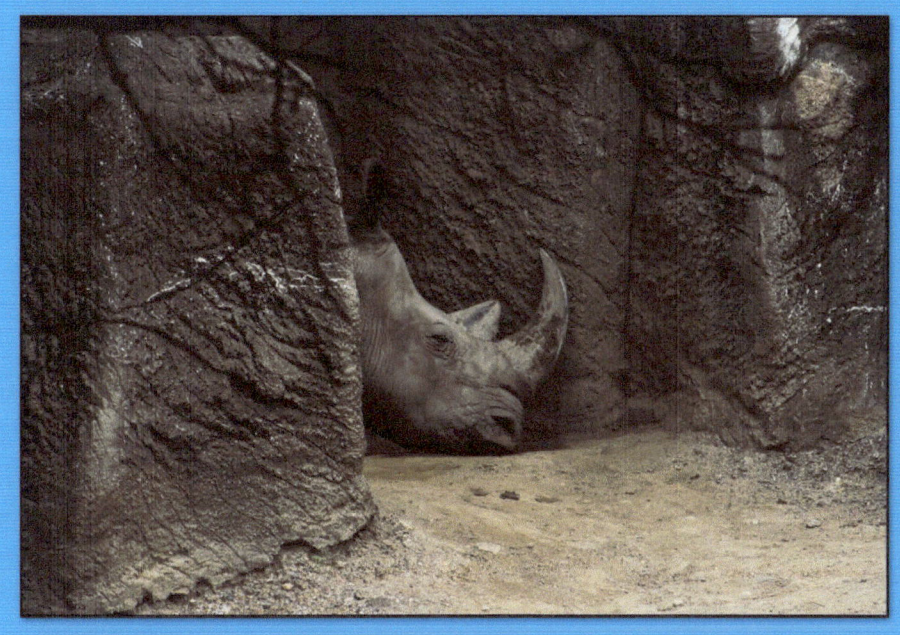

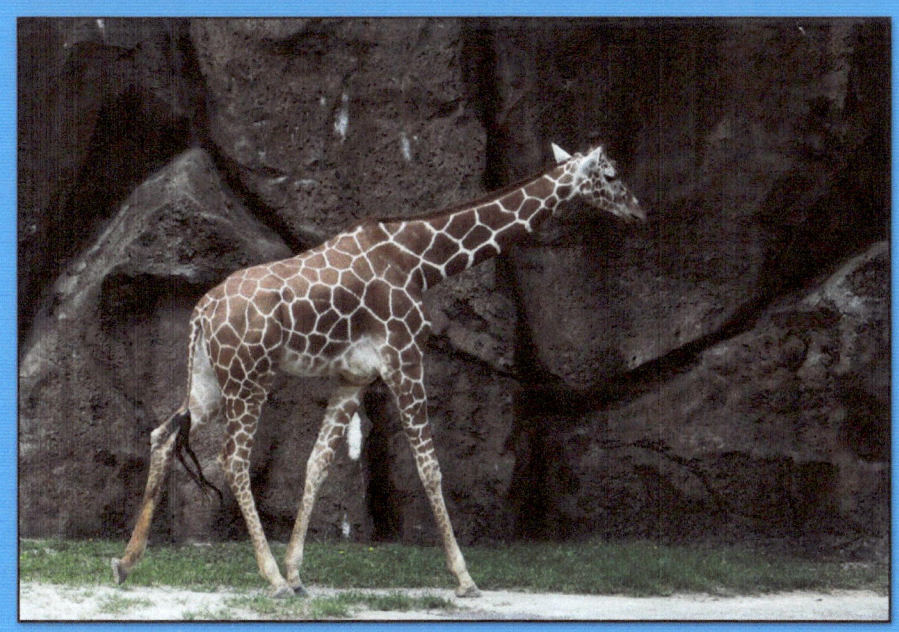

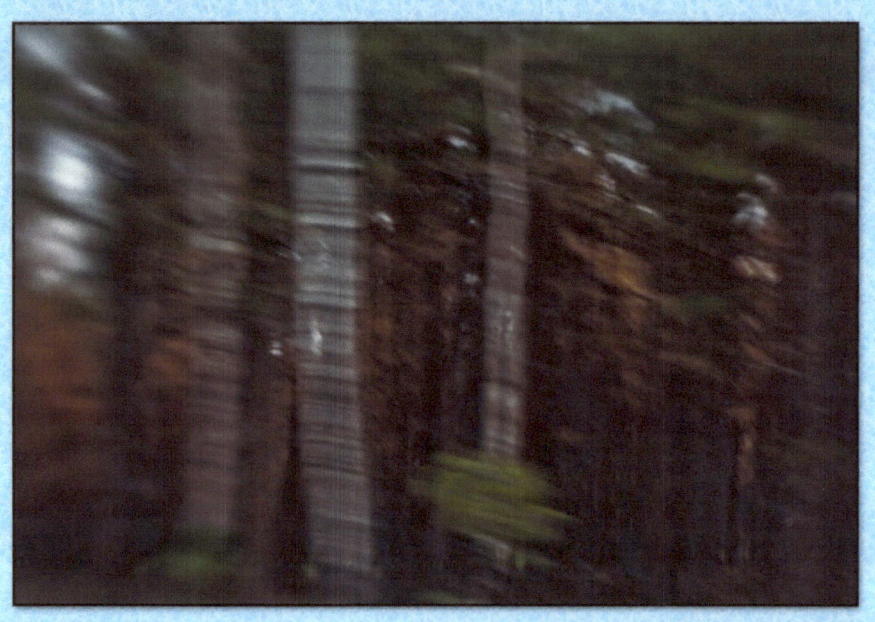

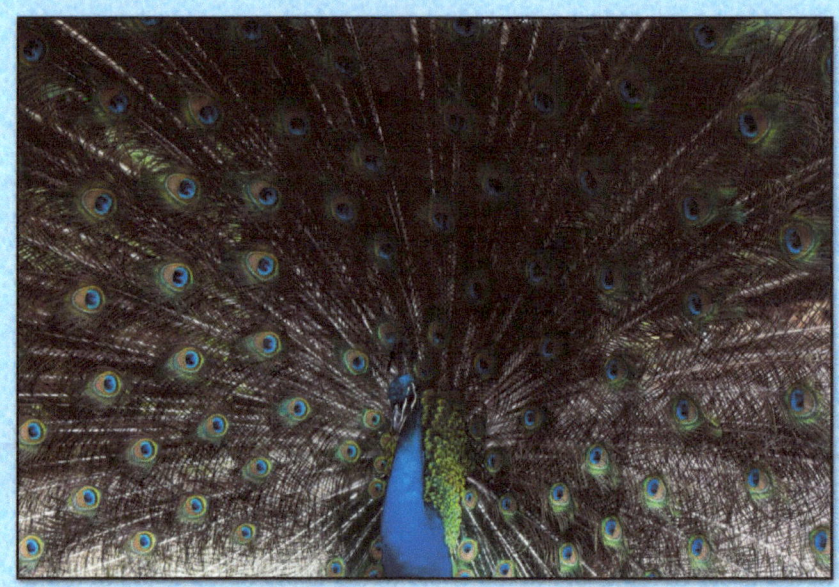

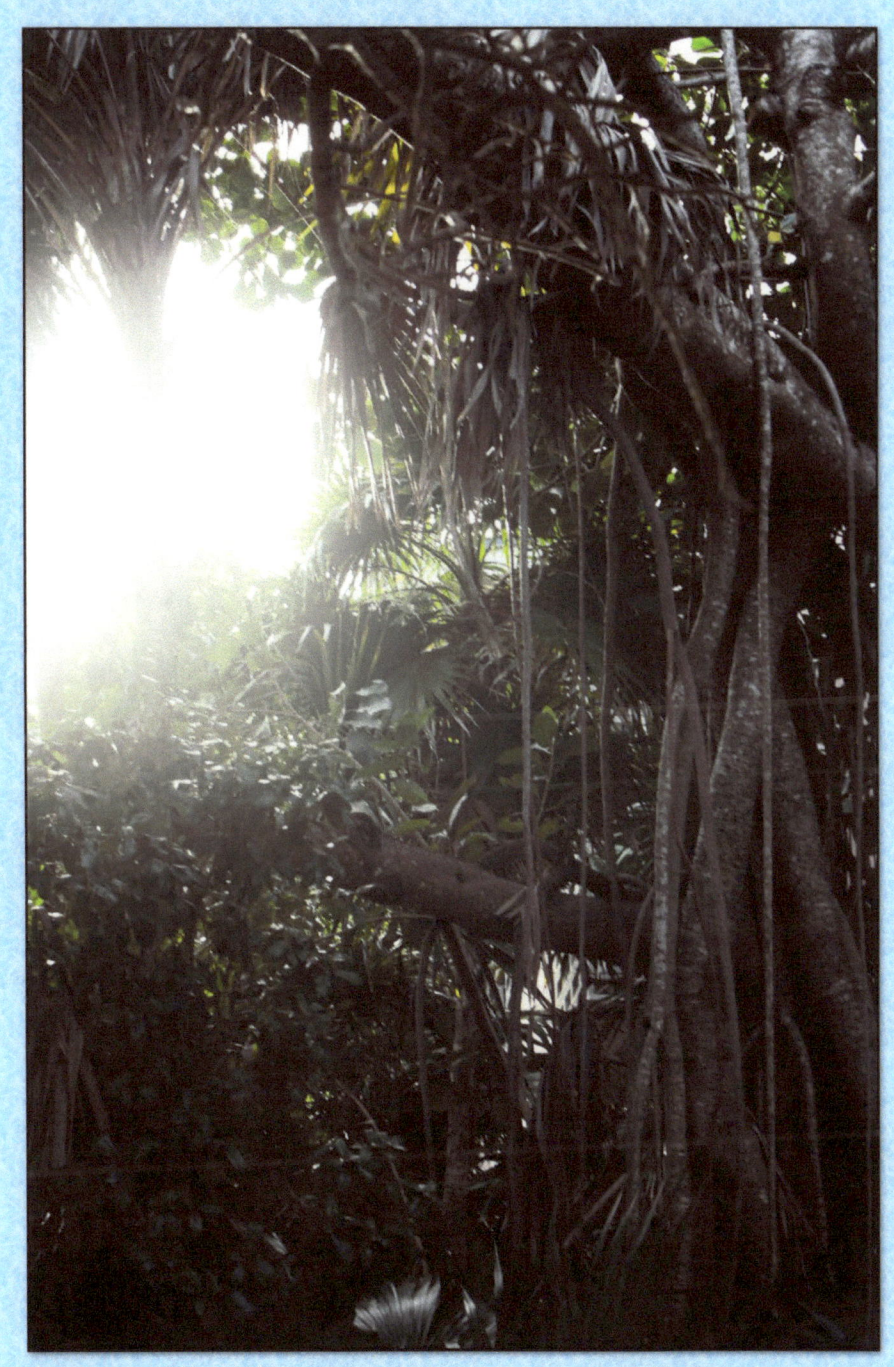

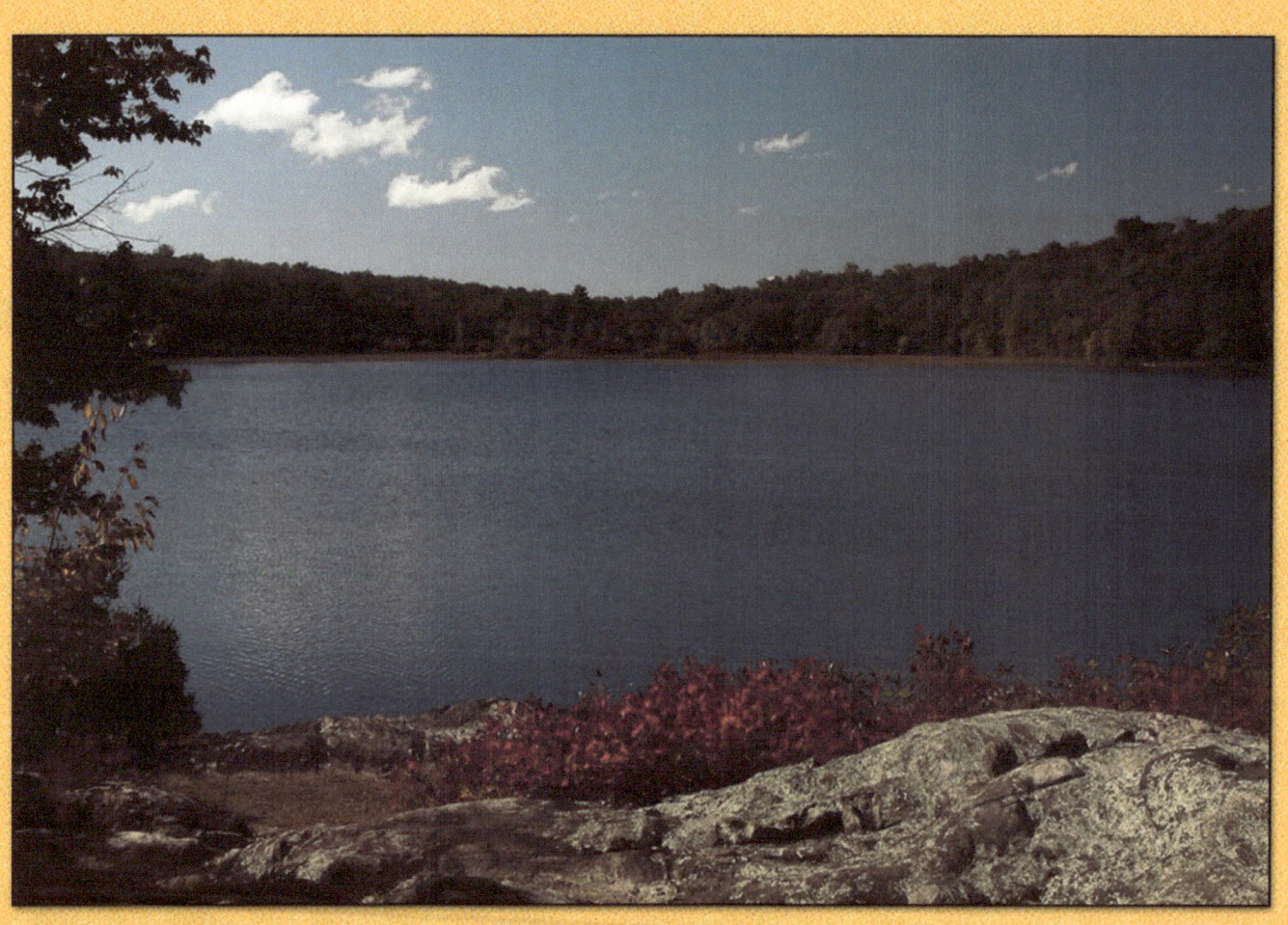

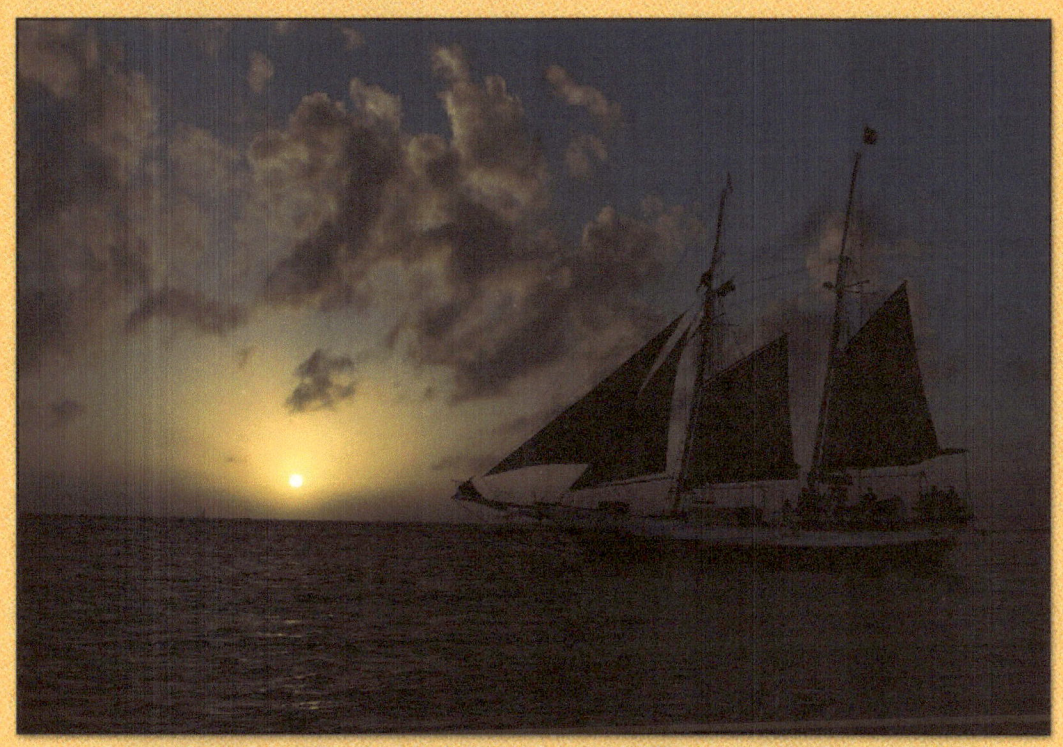

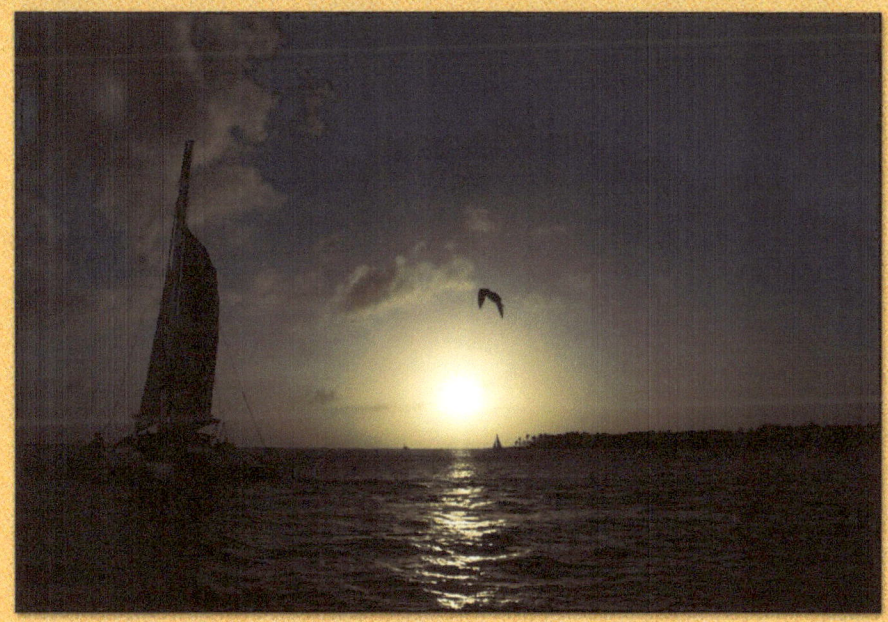

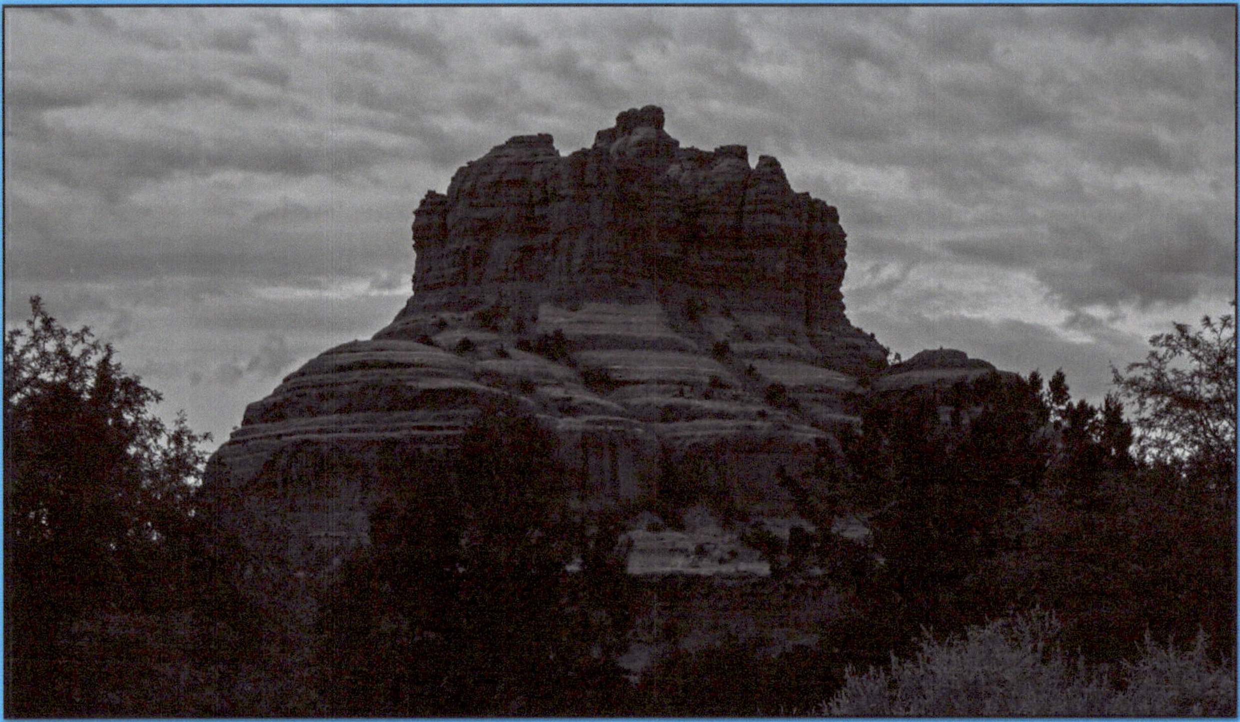

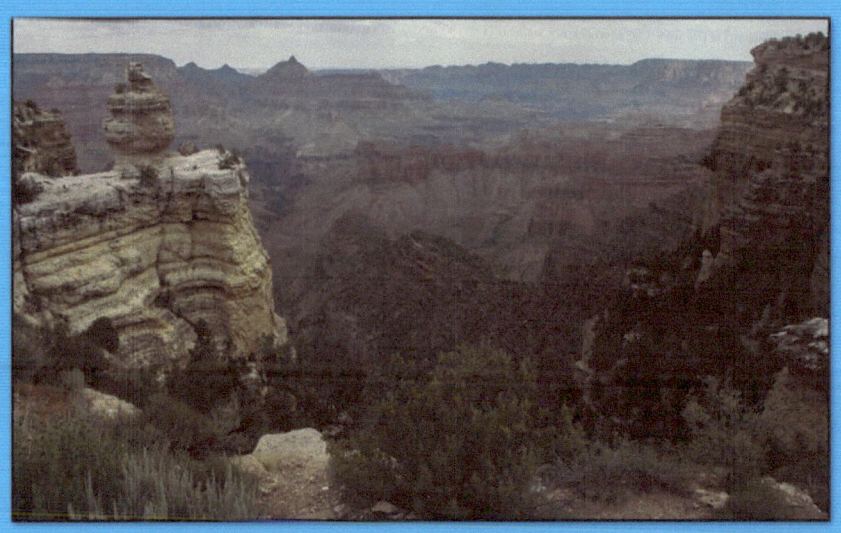

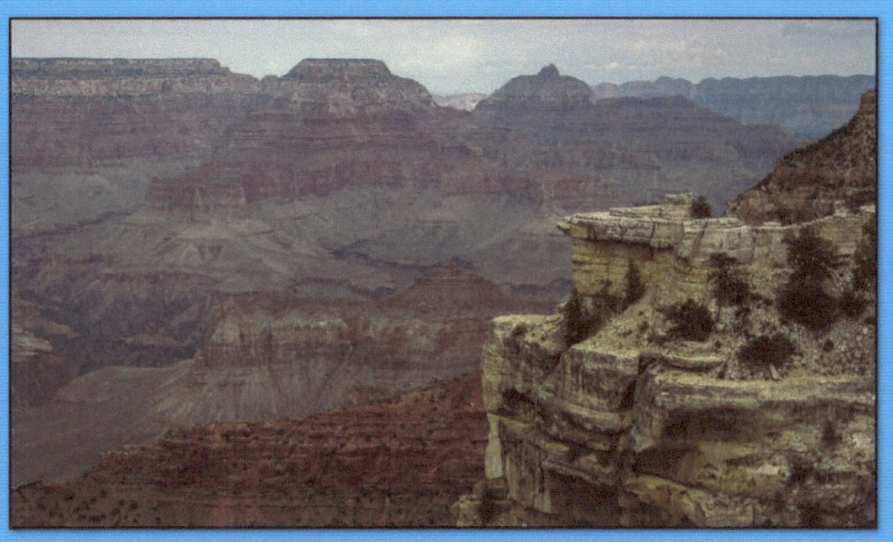

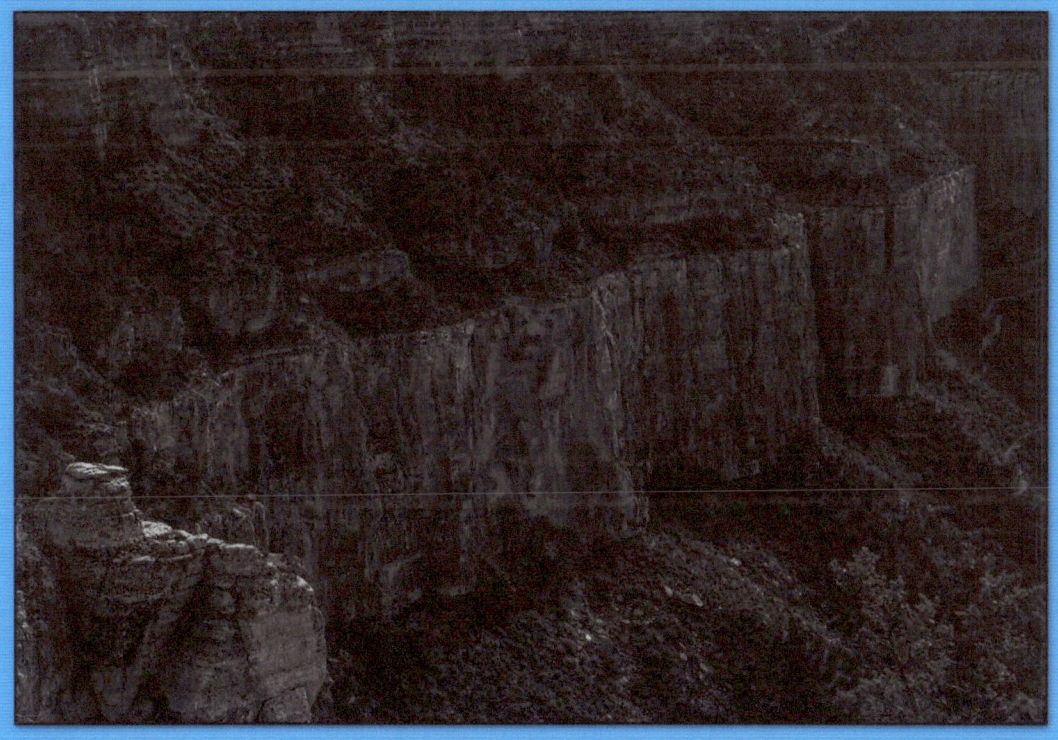

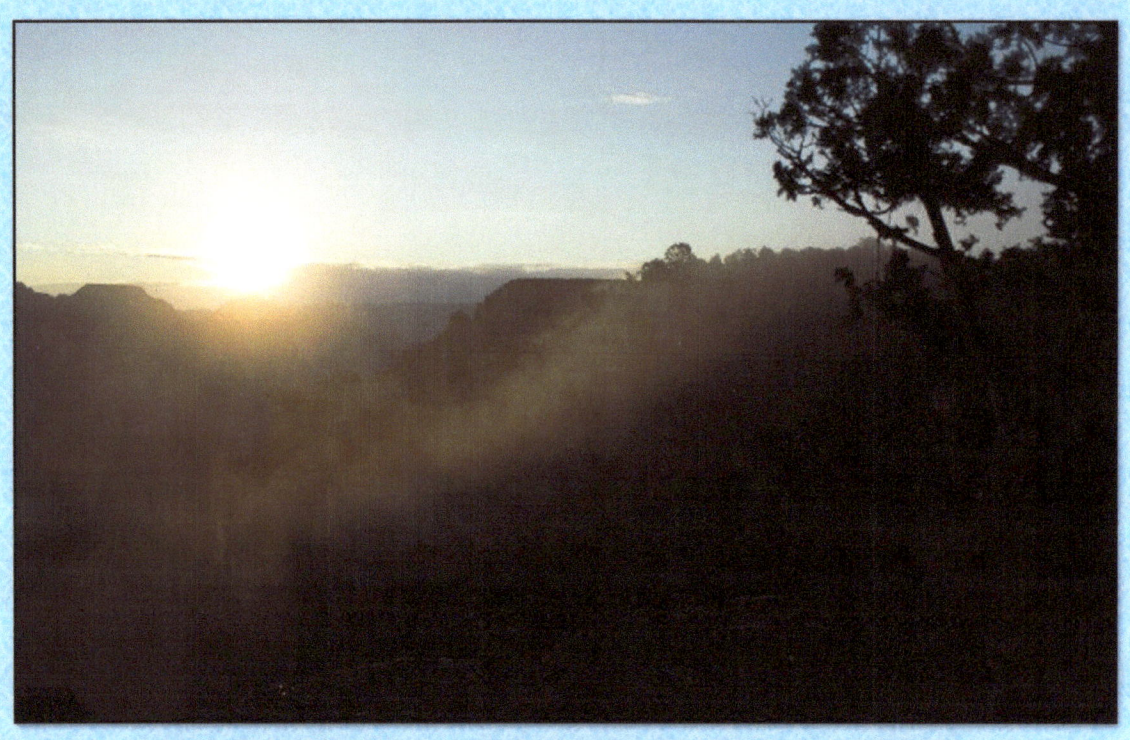

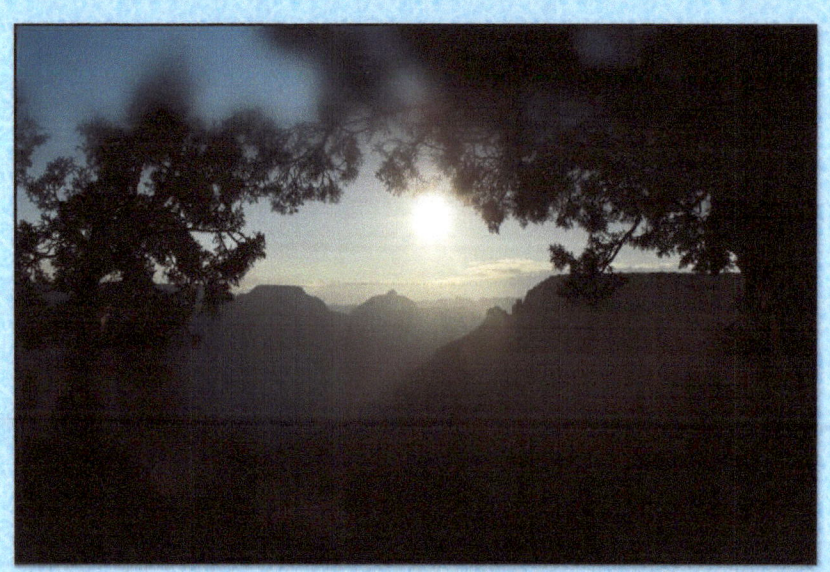

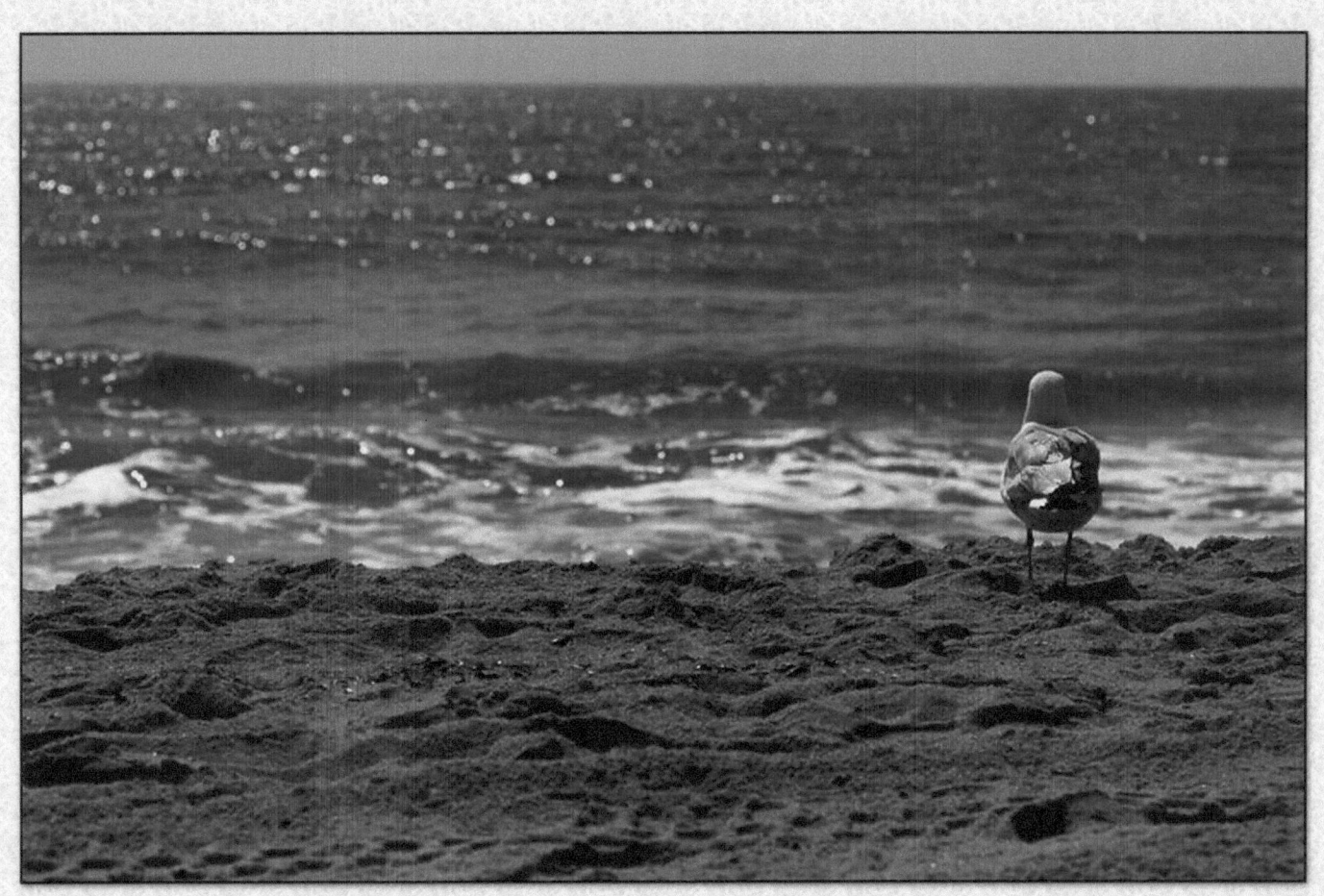

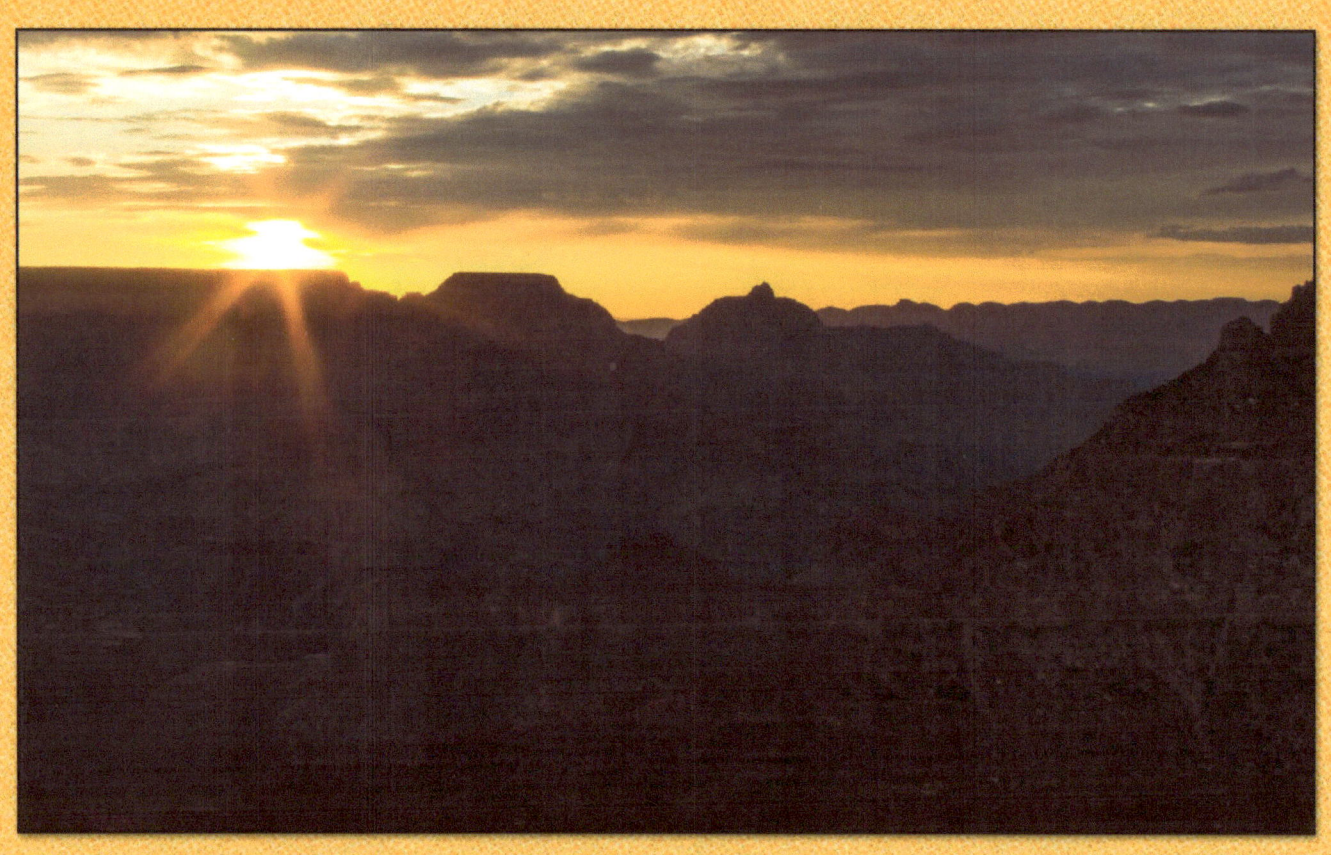

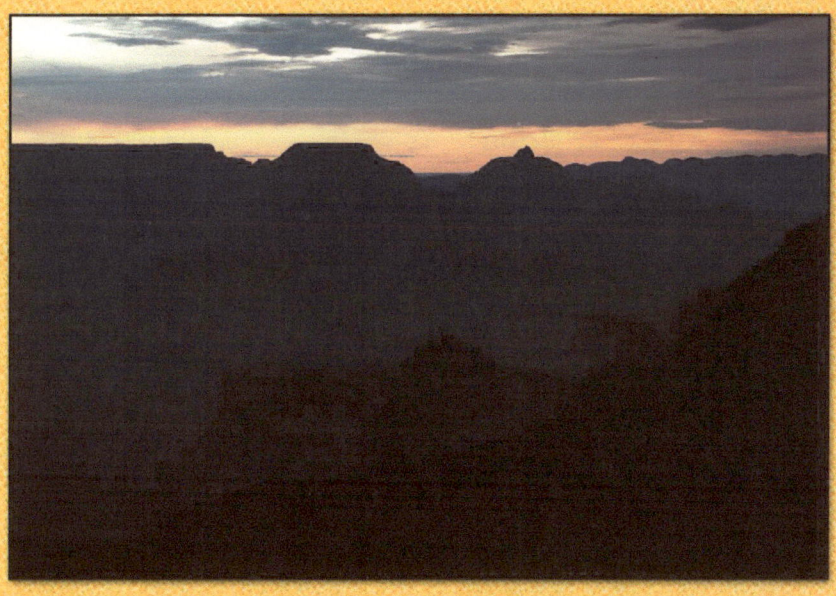

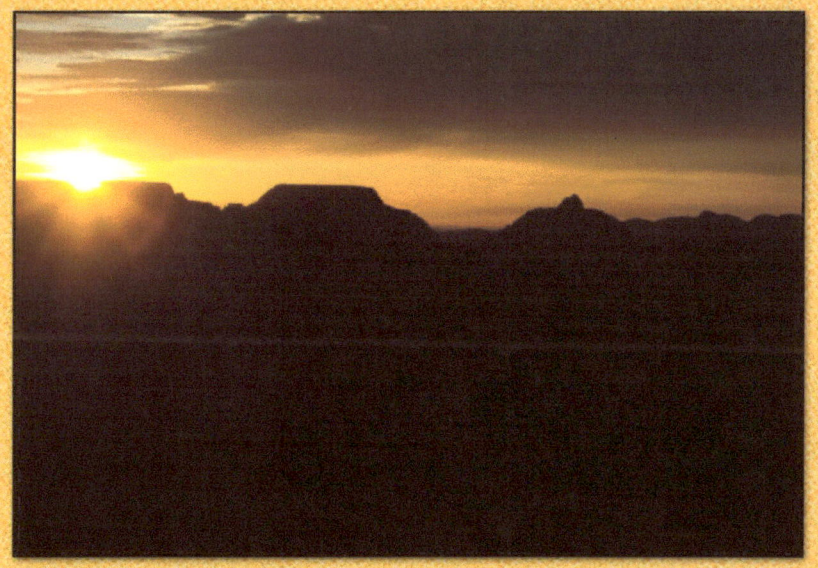

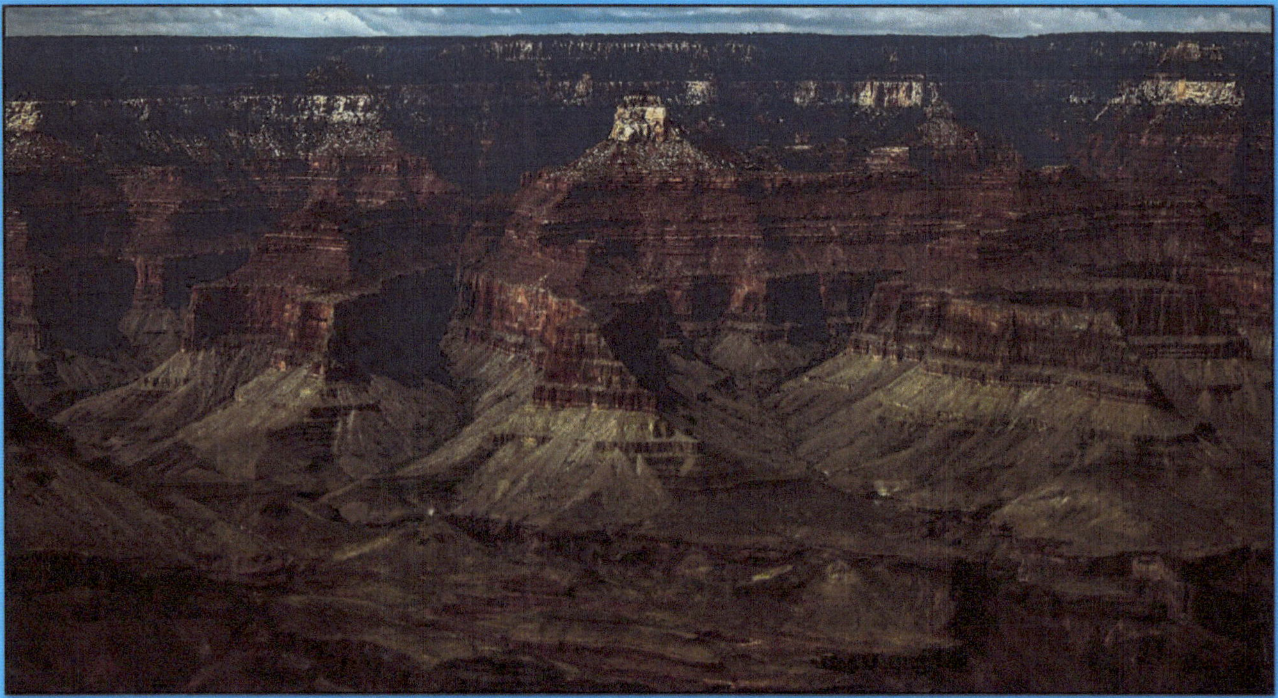

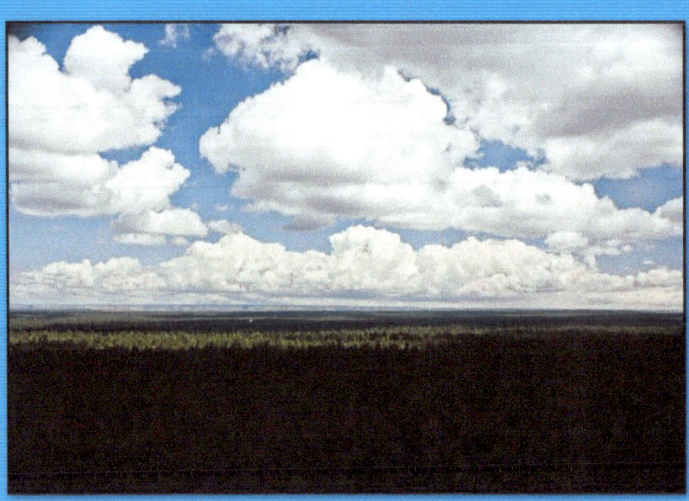
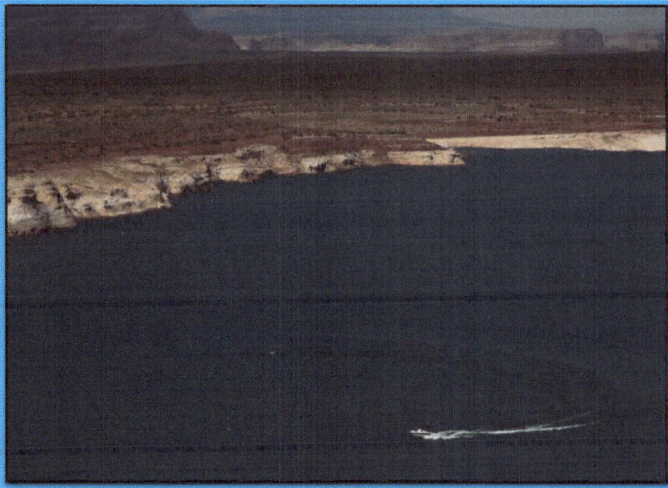

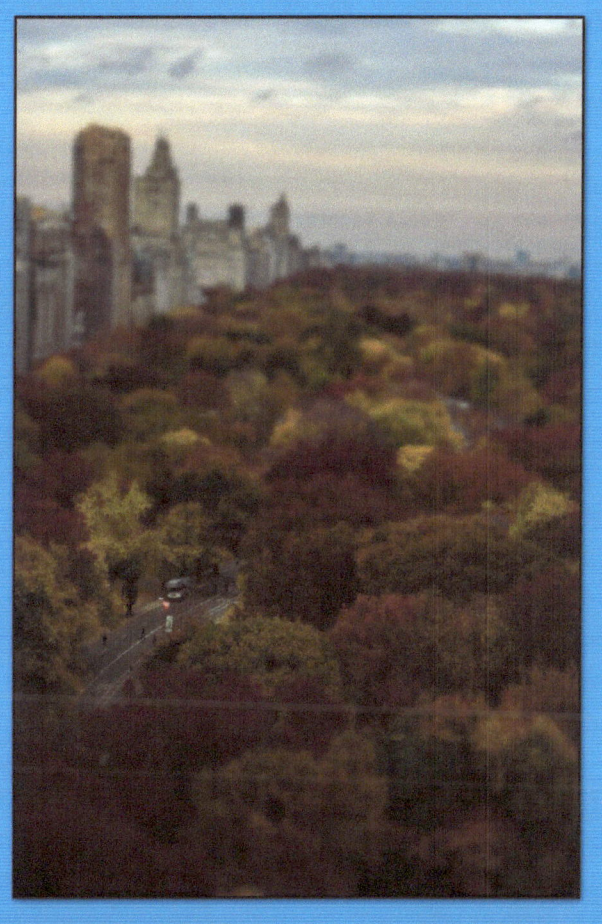

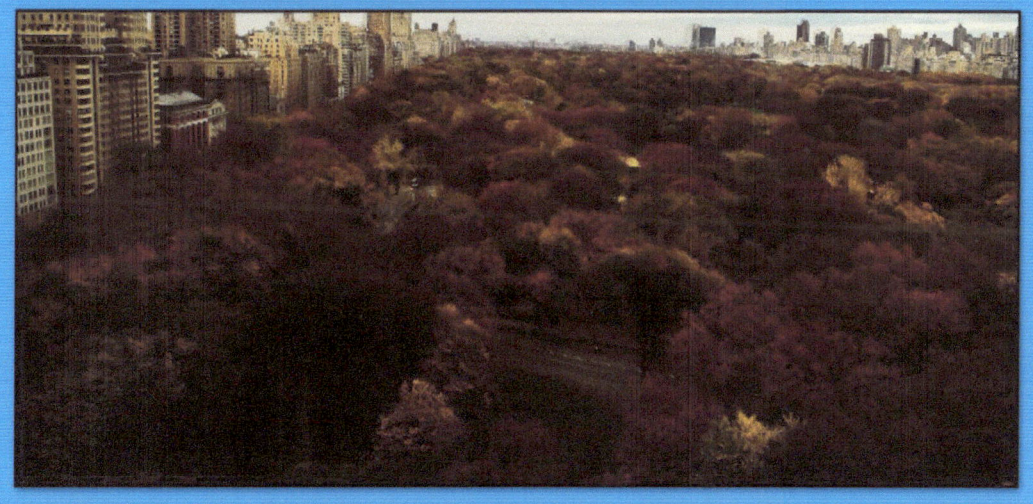

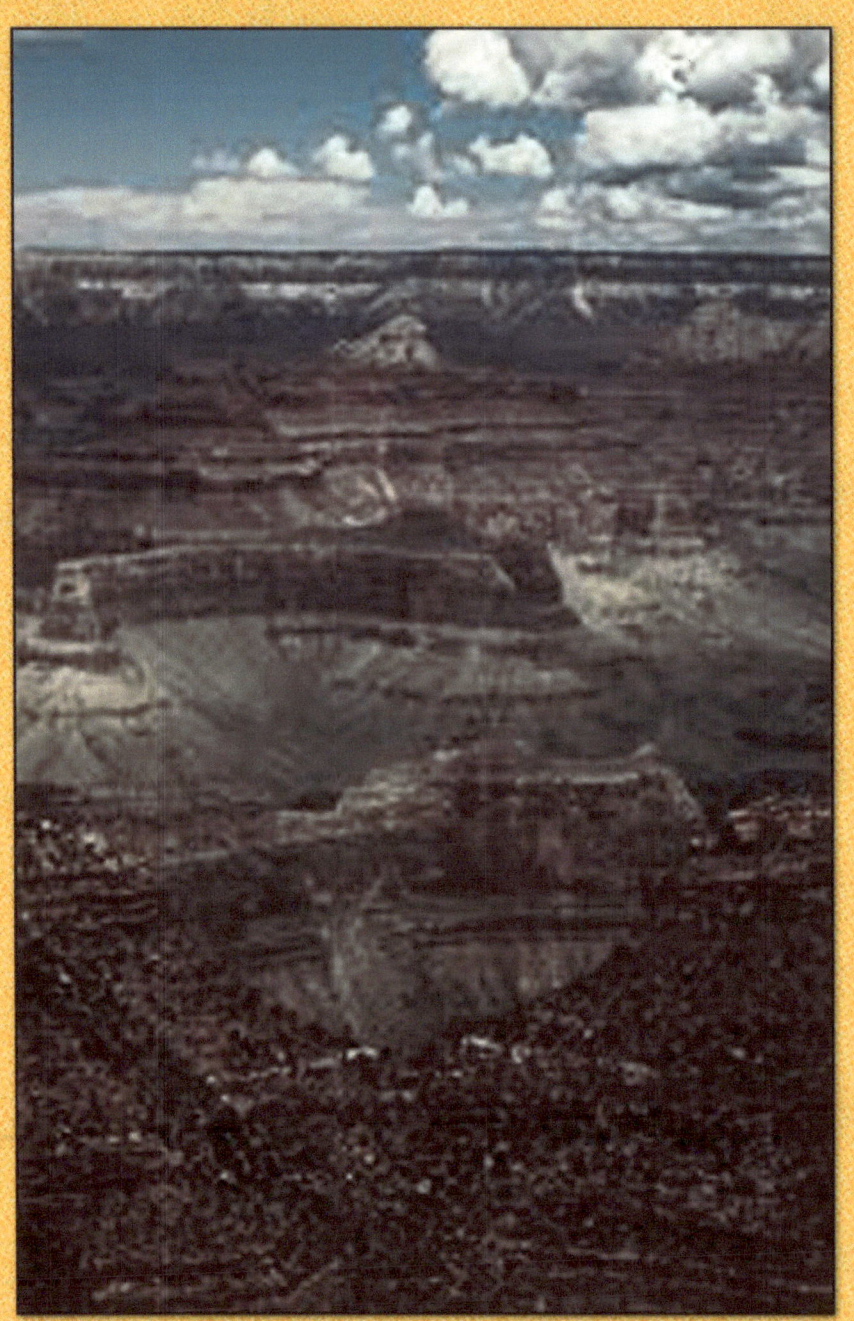

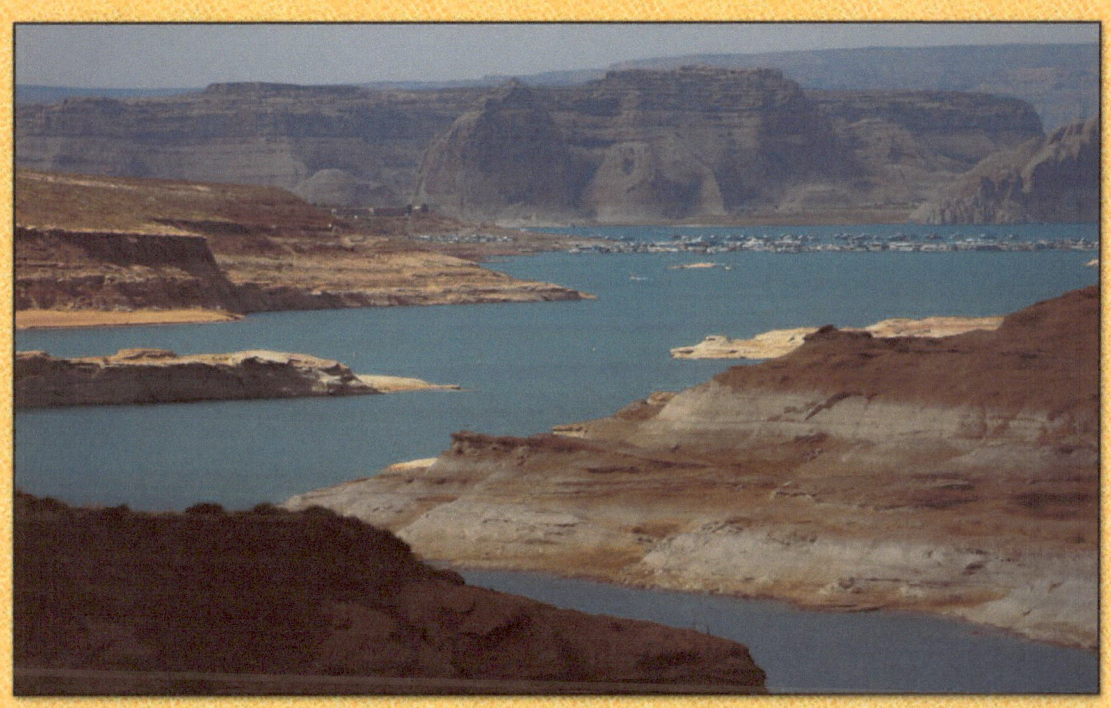
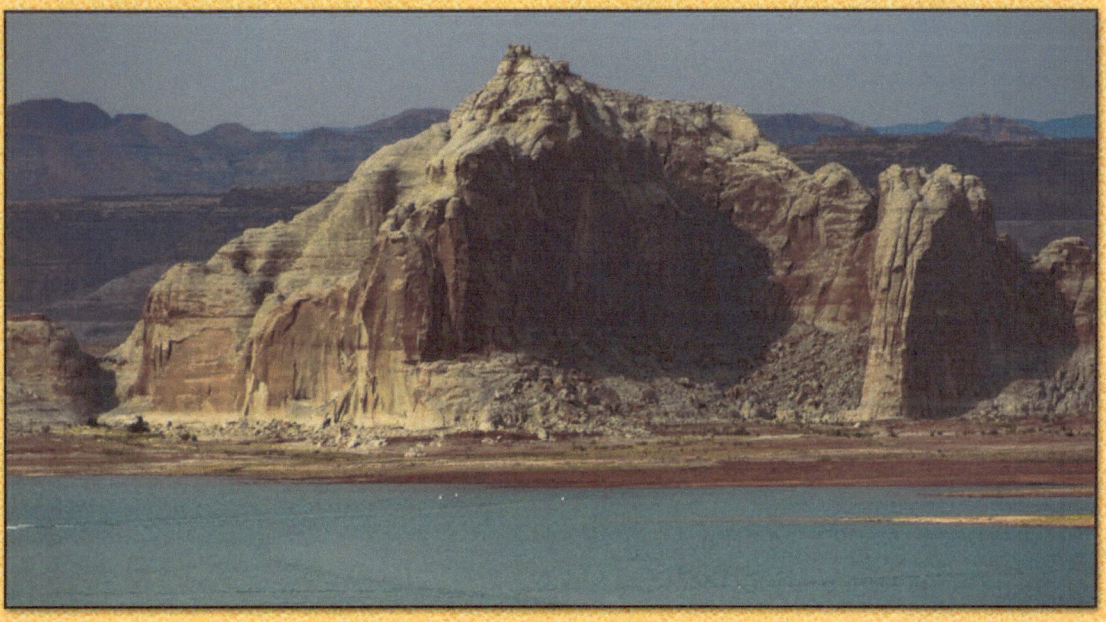

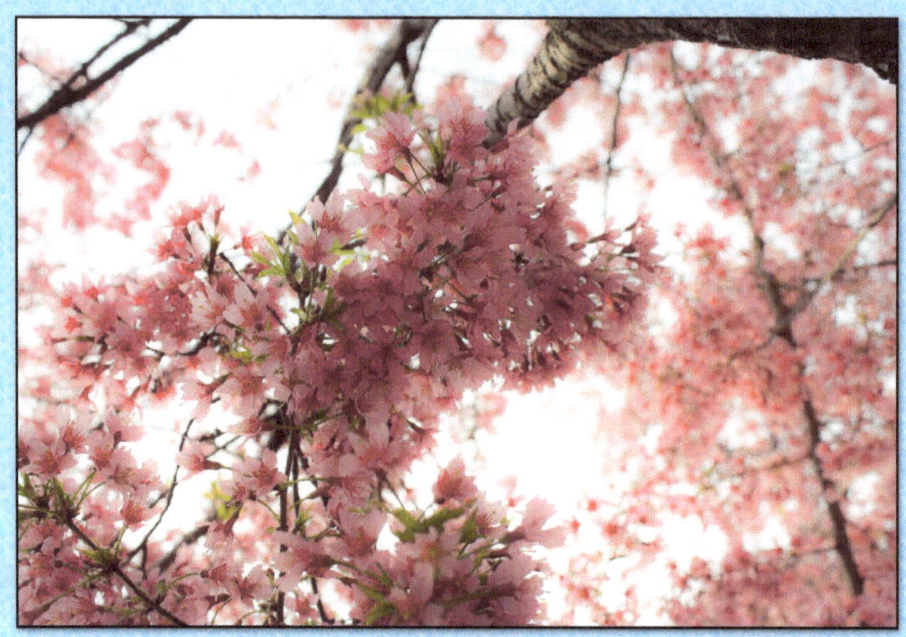

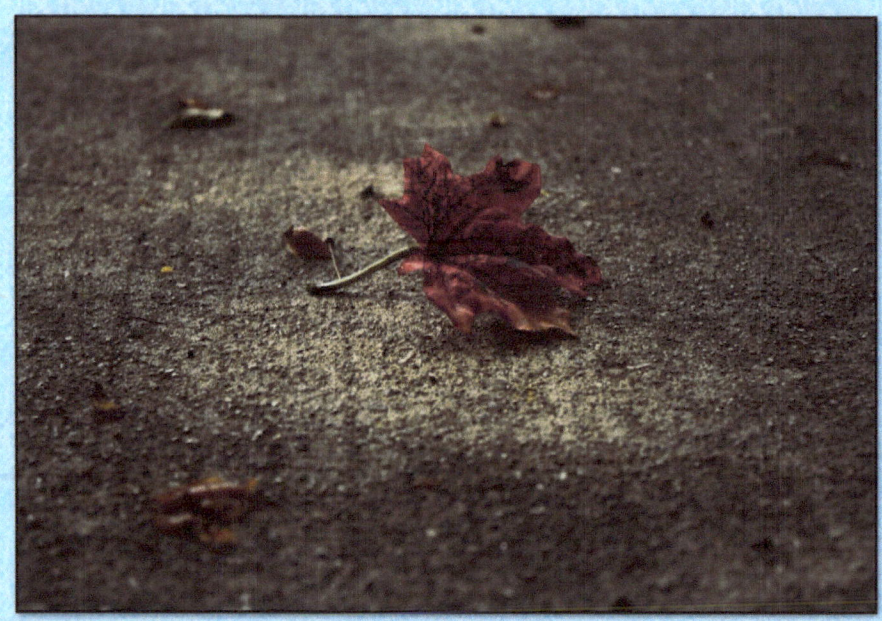

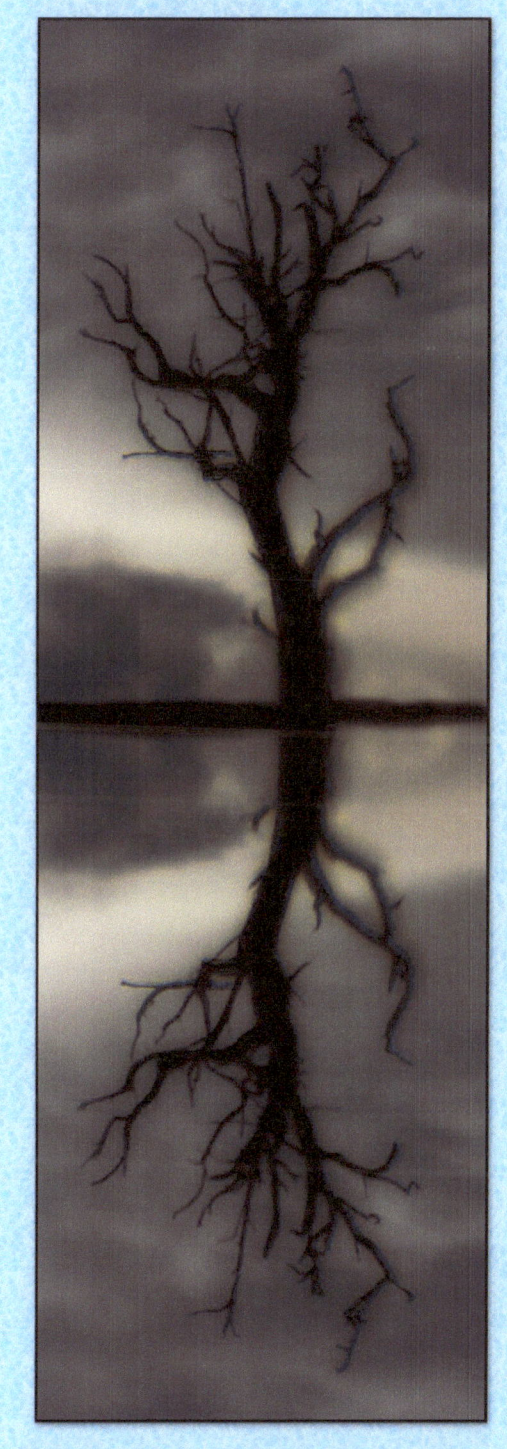

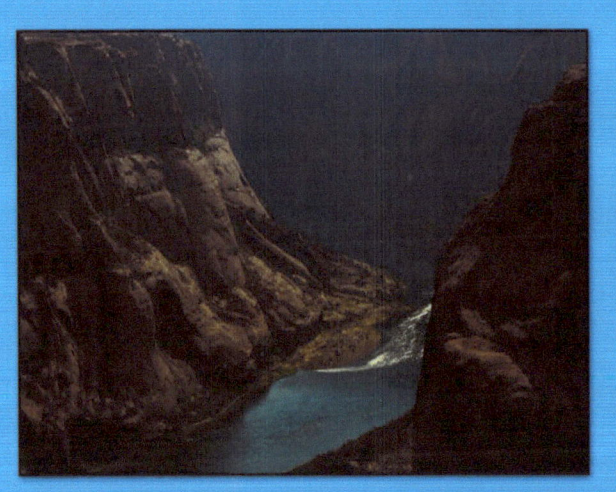
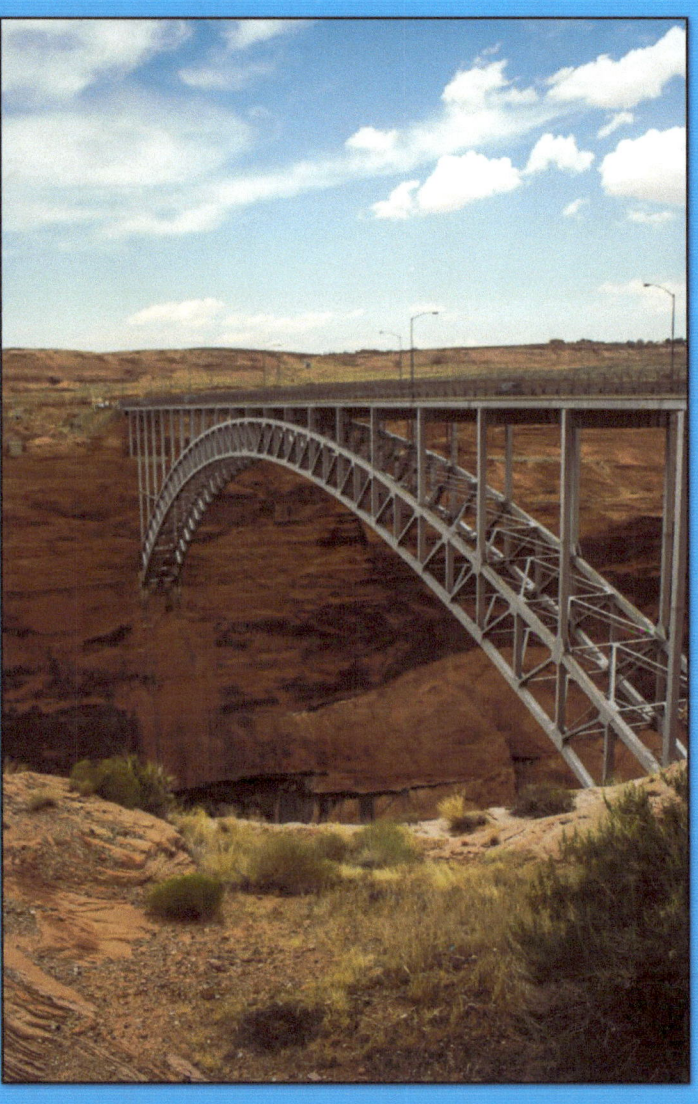

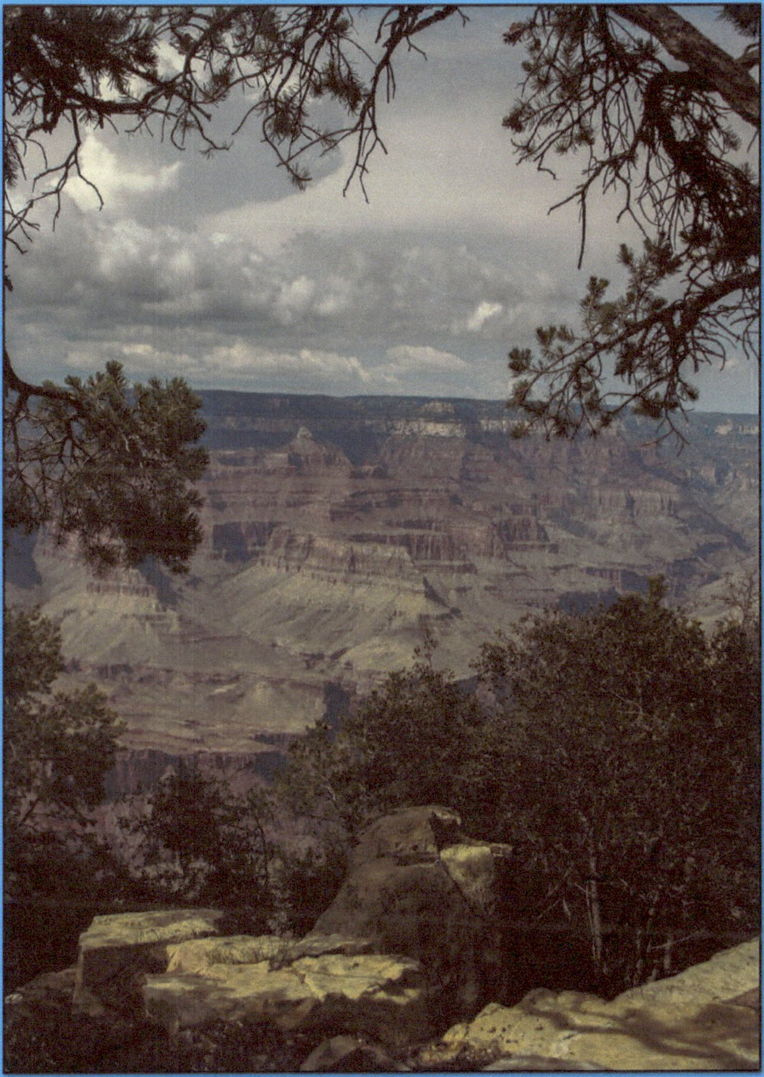

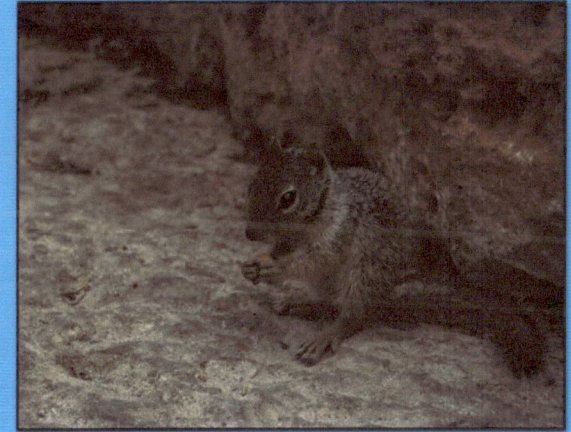

Now Go Outside and Enjoy Nature for Yourself!

I Hope you enjoyed my book and I hope it encourages you to embrace all that nature has to offer us. So put down the kindle or close this book and please, go outside, nature is waiting.

My name is Kathleen Odenthal and I am a professional photographer. I started shooting by just wandering around outside and photographing everything that caught my eye. Before I knew it I was shooting weddngs, shooting commercials and opening my own studio.
Life is beautiful and the coolest thing is that we all view it differently. This is how I view the world, I hope you enjoyed.

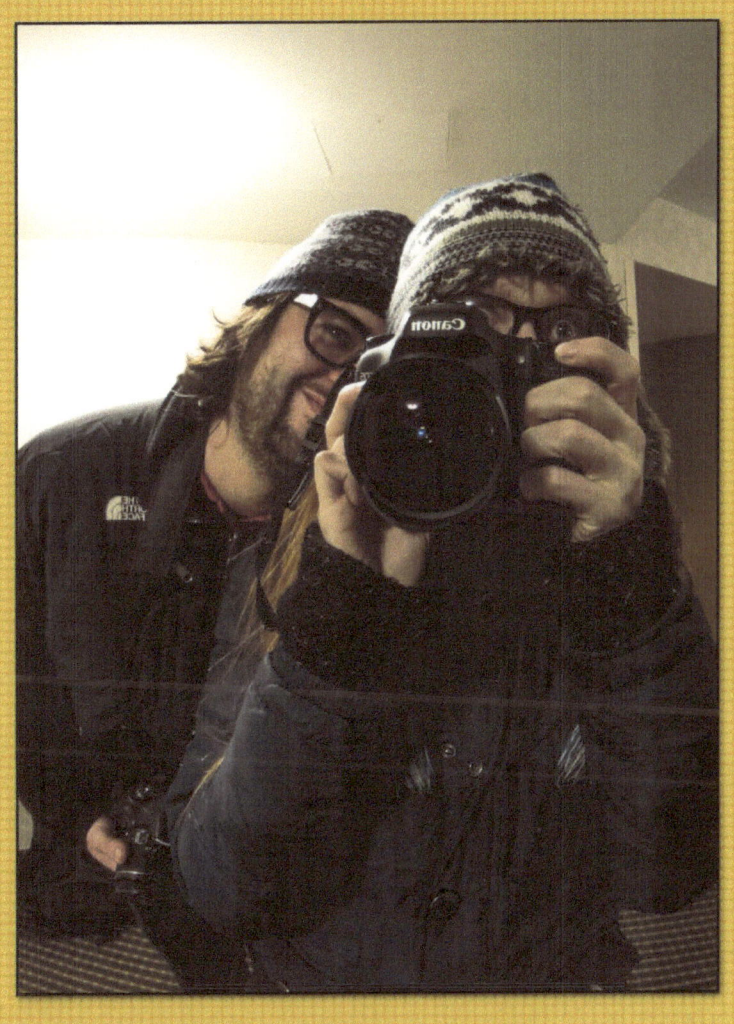

www.ingramcontent.com/pod-product-compliance
Lightning Source LLC
Chambersburg PA
CBHW050358180526
45159CB00005B/2069